HE LEO

A New Voice
Hawaiian Playwrights

Kāmau
Alani Apio

Kupua
Tammy Haili'ōpua Baker

Da Mayah
Lee Cataluna

Ka Wai Ola
Victoria Nalani Kneubuhl

**with introduction and commentary
by John H.Y. Wat and Meredith M. Desha**

ISBN 978-0-910043-66-3

This is issue #83 of *Bamboo Ridge, Journal of Hawai'i Literature and Arts* (ISSN 0733-0308).

Copyright © 2003 Bamboo Ridge Press

Published by Bamboo Ridge Press

Indexed in the American Humanities Index

Bamboo Ridge Press is a member of the Council of Literary Magazines and Presses (CLMP).

Cover and title page: "Green Ti" 2003, monotype by Mary Mitsuda; Hal Lum, photographer.

Photo credits: *Kāmau*: Ku'ulani Malia Littlejohn; *Da Mayah*: Brad Goda; *Kupua*: John H.Y. Wat; *Ka Wai Ola*: courtesy of the Honolulu Theatre for Youth

Typesetting, design, and graphics: Wayne Kawamoto

Bamboo Ridge Press is a nonprofit, tax-exempt corporation formed in 1978 to foster the appreciation, understanding, and creation of literary, visual, or performing arts by, for, or about Hawai'i's people. This project is supported in part by grants from the National Endowment for the Arts (NEA) and the State Foundation on Culture and the Arts (SFCA), celebrating over thirty years of culture and the arts in Hawai'i. The SFCA is funded by appropriations from the Hawai'i State Legislature and by grants from the NEA.

NATIONAL
ENDOWMENT
FOR THE ARTS

Bamboo Ridge is published twice a year. For subscription information, back issues, or a catalog, please contact:

Bamboo Ridge Press
P. O. Box 61781
Honolulu, HI 96839-1781
(808) 626-1481
www.bambooridge.org

9   8   22 23 24

CONTENTS

Introduction

J. Wat

When I began working on this special issue of *Bamboo Ridge*, I thought it obviously should have a Hawaiian title, but because my knowledge of Hawaiian language is limited, I asked Tammy Baker to suggest a name for this collection of plays. She and her husband came up with *He Leo Hou*, translated as "a new voice," which seems powerfully appropriate to me. While Hawaiians have always used artistic means of expression, traditionally in such forms as hula, chant, and storytelling, there is no exact parallel for the Western dramatic form in traditional Hawaiian performance genres. The writing and production of plays by Hawaiian writers is a relatively recent development and Western-style drama is therefore a new voice for Hawaiian artistic expression.

This is not to say that the four playwrights we have included in this collection are necessarily the first writers of Hawaiian ancestry to have plays produced and published. When the short list of playwrights was making its way around the literary grapevine, Lee Tonouchi, "da Pidgin Guerrilla," e-mailed us that we could hardly overlook the work of Tremaine Tamayose. While we have not had the opportunity to publish a complete play by Tamayose, we have, in *Bamboo Ridge* issue number ten, published excerpts from *Big Boys Don't Cry* and *Onolulu*.

Still there has been a significant increase in the number of Hawaiian writers using the Western dramatic form in the last decade as well as in the number of plays by Hawaiian writers produced on local stages and published as single volumes and in anthologies. Plays by Hawaiian writers have been produced by, among others, Diamond Head Theatre, the University of Hawai'i Kennedy Theatre, the University of Hawai'i at Hilo, and Honolulu Theatre for Youth (HTY), with most produced by Kumu Kahua Theatre.

Three of the plays included in this volume, Alani Apio's *Kāmau*, Tammy Baker's *Kupua*, and Lee Cataluna's *Da Mayah* were first produced at Kumu Kahua. Victoria Kneubuhl's *Ka Wai Ola* was commissioned and produced by HTY.

In addition to the plays printed here, Kumu Kahua has produced *Kāmau A'e*, Apio's sequel to *Kāmau*; Cataluna's *Ulua, the Musical*; *Aloha Friday*; and *Super Secret Squad*; as well as Kneubuhl's *The Conversion of Ka'ahumanu*, *Ka'iulani: A Cantata for Theatre* (co-authored with Ryan Page, Robert Nelson, and Dennis Carroll), *Emmalehua*, and *Ola Na Iwi*. Kumu Kahua also produced *Ola Ka Lau* by Kimo Armitage and *The Season of Yellow Ginger* by Margaret Jones.

Each of the four playwrights chosen for this anthology has a significant body of produced work seen by a wide range of audiences. Apio's *Kāmau* has played to neighbor island audiences in addition to its extended Honolulu run. Baker's work includes several Hawaiian language plays, produced with her company Kā Hālau Hanakeaka, which ran in several different venues throughout the state. Cataluna's prolific output has been presented by at least four companies in a number of different spaces including a production of *Da Mayah* on Maui and more recently a production of *You Somebody* at Diamond Head Theatre. Kneubuhl's extensive body of work has been produced and presented in Hawai'i, on the mainland, and internationally. Kumu Kahua's international tour in 1990 took both *The Conversion of Ka'ahumanu* and *Ka'iulani* to Los Angeles and Washington D.C., and to the International Fringe Festival in Edinburgh, Scotland. *January 1893*, Kneubuhl's dramatic recreation of the events surrounding the overthrow of the Hawaiian monarchy, played out near the actual sites of the historical events as part of the centennial commemoration of the overthrow, was witnessed by tens of thousands.

Victoria Nalani Kneubuhl's contribution to this collection, *Ka Wai Ola*, is a play commissioned by HTY for an audience of fourth, fifth, and sixth graders. While the story seems geared for that age group, it examines complex issues of island conservation and water rights that concern all of Hawai'i's people while being of special interest to Native Hawaiians. And while Kneubuhl makes some concessions to the youth audience (the central characters are young people), she constructs her play using sophisticated dramatic structures evident in her other works.

Tammy Haili'ōpua Baker's *Kupua* is actually two short plays based on traditional Hawaiian stories but set in more contemporary times. Baker's retelling in contemporary Pidgin (Hawaiian Creole English), in contemporary settings, with contempary characters, in contemporary Western dramatic form, reinvigorates the ancient stories and makes it possible for contemporary audiences, those who do not understand Hawaiian, to understand, to appreciate, and to learn from them.

Kāmau by Alani Apio is the first part of an intended trilogy about a contemporary Hawaiian family. *Kāmau* introduces three cousins, Alika, Michael, and George, who constitute the center of an extended exploration into the lives of contemporary Hawaiian men. *Kāmau* focuses primarily on the story of Alika, the cousin who sacrifices his personal dreams and ambitions to ensure the welfare of his adopted family. *Kāmau A'e*, the second part of the trilogy focuses on the character of Michael and his coming into political consciousness during his time in prison and after his subsequent release.

Lee Cataluna's *Da Mayah* is a character-driven local comedy centered around the beleaguered and talented Sandralene Ferreira, who is the assistant to the ostensible mayor of Hilo. Cataluna's comedy is full of cultural jokes familiar to most local audiences. While being entertained, these audiences were gently prodded to look at themselves and at all of the recognizable small failings and successes that make up the lives of all of us who live in Hawai'i.

This side-by-side comparison of the plays demonstrates the breadth and variety of styles and genres that these play-wrights work in and explore. While this wide range of ideas and genres might make it seem that there are few commonalities, there is some element of what it is to be Hawaiian in contemporary society that is embedded in each of the works and in the writing practice of each of the playwrights.

Baker and Apio's writings are the most consciously Hawaiian. Baker's body of work includes plays in Hawaiian, English, and in Pidgin. She draws heavily from traditional sources; *Kupua* is a theatrical reworking of traditional *mo'olelo*. Apio's plays are consciously about the lives and challenges of Hawaiians forced to live in contemporary society. *Kāmau*, for example, is an explicit examination of the legacy of colonization for descendants of the indigenous people of Hawai'i, and specifically how contemporary Hawaiian men must often make unsung and heroic choices to deal with the loss of cultural values that result from colonization.

While several of Kneubuhl's plays focus on Hawaiians and Hawaiian issues, not all do. The Hawaiian elements of Kneubuhl's plays are less or more evident based on her subject matter. *Ka Wai Ola* is a play that is very much about Hawaiian issues. It is a play about water rights, an issue that concerns everyone in our island culture, but it is also a play that specifically concerns Hawaiians, both because the ways that govern how water is used have always been an integral part of traditional cultural practice for Hawaiians and because the economic well-being of contemporary Hawaiians often depends on the governance of water.

Cataluna's plays seem on the surface to be the least explicitly Hawaiian. Instead they might be characterized as espousing a "local" aesthetic, with Pidgin sprinkled throughout and character types that audiences often take as their own: "That's my uncle." However in the polyglot and polyethnic character types of her plays there always seem to be one or more central characters who are, as audiences implicitly assume, part Hawaiian. And the clues to that identity, if not explicit as in a Hawaiian surname, are found in Hawaiian given names or in a concern or knowledge of Hawaiian ideology, ideals, and practices. Though these are not explicitly stated, a "local" audience would as easily recognize these characters as they would their own Hawaiian relatives. And in the contemporary culture of Hawai'i, this is often the case, that we are all related to someone Hawaiian, if not by blood, then by marriage.

Kneubuhl is at present perhaps the most acccomplished of the four playwrights included here. As a playwright of Samoan, Hawaiian, and Caucasian ancestry, Kneubuhl has over the course of her career been unafraid to tackle a range of subject matter while utilizing different dramatic styles, genres, and structures in her plays. For an illuminating discussion of the depth and breadth of Kneubuhl's work, see Craig Howes's introductory essay to her recently released collection, *Hawai'i Nei, Island Plays* (University of Hawai'i Press, 2002).

Tammy Haili'ōpua Baker, a teacher of Hawaiian language and culture, is perhaps best known as a playwright/director for her Hawaiian language plays produced by her company, Kā Hālau Hanakeaka. She invigorates the Hawaiian language by having it spoken in new forms. The tragedy, comedy, political satire, children's theatre, and the dramatization of traditional stories that characterize Baker's works are taking the Hawaiian language in new directions. While promoting the learning and understanding of Hawaiian language is part of her work, another part involves sharing

Hawaiian culture with those who do not understand the language, through her works in English or Pidgin.

Lee Cataluna makes her living by writing. Widely known as a newscaster, she now writes a regular column for *The Honolulu Advertiser*. She has also been a comedy writer for some of the seminal comedy groups in Hawai'i. Her theatrical output began with *Da Mayah*, in a play writing workshop taught by Kneubuhl and sponsored by Kumu Kahua. Since then, a prolific Cataluna has created new works every year which are highly comical and very specifically focused on the comedy of the "local" people of Hawai'i. While always funny, her plays also deal with serious contemporary issues, for example, the takeover of a local cable access television station by a mainland corporation in *Aloha Friday*, or the problems of child abuse in *Super Secret Squad*.

Alani Apio has been among other things a Hawaiian craftsman working with traditional materials, but he has more recently focused on corporate and community work. While writing is not the major focus of Apio's professional career, his plays are an integral part of his work and life as a contemporary Hawaiian man and reflect his compelling interest in trying to define what it is to be Hawaiian, especially as it applies to Hawaiian men, in the contemporary culture of the state.

So while *He Leo Hou* represents a new voice, the artistic expression of Hawaiian writers in a traditionally Western genre, it is a voice already speaking with great power and distinction. The four playwrights represented in this collection are still active in producing new and groundbreaking work and although they probably are the most notable and well-known members of the community of Hawaiian playwrights, they are not alone. Audiences should look forward to hearing from these and other playwrights of Hawaiian ancestry and seeing their works on stages locally, nationally, and internationally.

Finally, as is the caution in any printed anthology of plays, the reader would do well to remember that plays are written to be played out on a stage. While the plays printed here are worthy of study and discussion, the nuances of spoken language and performance they embody only live fully on the stage; this is especially true of plays that incorporate Hawaiian language and Pidgin. It is my hope that the reader will have an opportunity to see and hear these and other plays in full production.

Kumu Kahua Theatre Presents The Annual Neighbor Island Tour

KĀMAU*

World Premiere of a Play by Alani Apio
Directed by Harry Wong III

O'AHU
Kumu Kahua Theatre
8:00 pm
May 20, 21, 27, 28
July 1, 2
6:30 pm
May 22*, 29, July 3
*Signed for the hearing impaired

WAI'ANAE HIGH SCHOOL
7:00 pm
June 10, 11
Reservations for all
O'ahu Performances:
737-4161

MAUI
Maui Community College
Student Lounge
7:30 pm
June 3, 4
Maui Ticket Inquiries:
875-2460

HILO, HAWAII
UHH Theatre, Hilo
7:30 pm
June 17, 18
2:00 pm;
June 18, 19
Hilo Ticket Inquiries:
933-3350

LIHUE, KAUA'I
Island School Main Hall
7:30 pm:
June 24, 25
Lihue Ticket Inquiries:
245-3408

KAINALIU, HAWAI'I
Aloha Theatre
8:00 pm:
July 8, 9
Kainaliu Ticket Inquiries:
322-9924

ADMISSION:
$8 Adults.
$6 Seniors, Students,
Children, Groups of 10 or
more reserving in advance.
$5 Wai'anae show only.

kāmau: 1: to keep on, continue,
persevere. 2. to drink, especially
intoxicants; a toast, somewhat like "to
your health." 3. card game; trumps; to trump.

KĀMAU Season Sponsors: Jeff Crabtree, Attorney; Office of Hawaiian Affairs; State Foundation on Culture and the Arts through appropriations from the Legislature of the State of Hawai'i; MAUI Sponsor: MCC CCECS and VITEC-BIDS; HILO Sponsor: UHH Performing Arts; KAUA'I Sponsor: Kaua'i Community Players; KAINALIU Sponsor: Aloha Performing Arts Center

Kāmau:
Sacrifice and Collaboration
M. Desha

According to Harry Wong III, Alani Apio's *Kāmau* is "an unsafe play."

"This play is not what you would think of as a 'Hawaiian' play. The depiction of Hawaiians can be quite unflattering. This play airs dirty laundry, and leaves it out there for everyone to see. Consequences are shown, and it all rings true," Wong comments.

Though at times unflinching, the landscape Apio depicts is one deeply rooted in his own experience: the death of Hawaiian men close to him. "By the time I got into college, a number of my friends and family had killed themselves. What I went through, dealing with that, had left me feeling, at times, deep anger and despair. I wrote *Kāmau* to figure out if there's a reason behind this."

Apio grew up on Oʻahu in the late 1960s and early 1970s, "when Ewa Beach was still surrounded by sugar cane," he says. "My dad taught me to fish—not as a living, but to provide for our family. We were poor in a Western sense, but rich in family and spirituality. In writing, I realized the ways I was taught to be as a Hawaiian man didn't jibe with what I was taught to be as an American citizen."

For Wong, who directed the original production at Kumu Kahua Theatre in 1994, the play had a familiar resonance. "I felt the play was about my dad's generation. He was a surfer who kept his shorts in the back of his Hawaiian Tel truck, just in case there was a good break," Wong remembers. "My dad had other interests, but he put those aside to take care of his family.

Because of him, and others like him, people are able to say today, 'Us Hawaiians have to do this,' and, 'Us Hawaiians have to learn that.' But where were they when we needed to put food on the table?"

As *Kāmau* went into production, Wong pushed him to rewrite certain sections, especially the ending. "Bunches of stuff were hard for him to write. Alani was writing a strong play, and I encouraged him not to censor himself. Conversations would go like this:

"I would ask, 'What is Alika going to do?'

"Alani would reply, 'He shouldn't go back to the tour company.'

"'What is Alika going to do?'

"'But I don't—'

"'What is Alika going to do?'

"'He goes back.' And that's exactly what happens."

Apio concurs. "The last scenes of the play weren't finalized, and the ending only came about through a cumulative effort with Harry and the cast." The last scene evolved from a warm-up exercise. It was important in production to have the intensity build as pressures mount on Alika. Wong asked each person to pick the favorite line their character says, and their favorite line from the whole play.

The actors verbally surround Alika with these lines, illustrating how he's weighed down by responsibilities. Alika is without respite, and "his thoughts should be relentless," Wong says.

Nowhere was the theme of sacrifice coupled with collaborative stagecraft more effectively than the final moments. Israel Kamakawiwoʻole's "Mehameha/White Sandy Beach" plays softly as Alika dons his uniform again, and, goes back to work for the tour company. "After opening night, we decided Alika should not be defeated at the end by his decision," Wong says, drawing on his own observations of his father's generation for inspiration. "During production, the play was heartwrenching to watch. I remember after one show, three haole ladies were sitting in the theatre, crying. When I asked them why, one said, 'I don't know why I'm crying, but I can't stop.' People were actually calling out to him from the audience, not to go back to his job."

"It depends on where in Hawai'i you grew up," Apio notes. "Because loss and clash of culture didn't happen in a clean sweep across the Islands. And it's still happening."

"There are no 'evil haoles' or clear bad guys in this play, but you do feel a sense of tragedy," Wong says. "This is the kind of play where, ideally, you get to the end of it and you say, "You must change your life."

Ginger Gohier, Brian Wake, Charles Timtim.

KĀMAU

BY

ALANI APIO

with assistance from:

Harry Luke Wong III

Margaret Ann Leilani Jones

and John H.Y. Wat

Kāmau was first produced by Kumu Kahua Theatre for their 1994 Summer tour. It was directed by Harry Luke Wong III, with Margaret Ann Leilani Jones as assistant director and John H. Y. Wat as dramaturge. The original cast was as follows:

ALIKA KALEIHA'AHEO'ONĀKŪPUNA KEALOHA . . Charles Kūpahu Timtim
MOM . . . . .Nyla L. Fujii
BOSS . . . . .Neal Milner
GEORGE MAHEKONA . . . . .Edward Dion Costa
MICHAEL MAHEKONA . . . . .Bryan Hiroshi Wake
MRS. YAMAMOTO . . . . .Lisa Ann Omoto
MABEL CLEMENTS . . . . .Kathy Welch
HENRY CLEMENTS . . . . .Neal Milner
LISA . . . . .Cheryl Bartlett Wagenseller
. . . . .Justina Mattos (understudy)
STEVIE KALEI MAHEKONA . . . . .Ginger Makanalani Gohier
BUILDING INSPECTOR . . . . .Henry 'Bulldog' Conaty
SECURITY GUARD . . . . .Henry 'Bulldog' Conaty

Kāmau A'e, the sequel, is now available in bookstores and directly from the publisher.

SCENE 1

(Voices offstage.)

LISA: *(vo)* Alika, what's the matter?

MICHAEL: *(vo)* We goin' be all right.

MRS. YAMAMOTO: *(vo)* You boys are going to be tested all your lives.

STEVIE: *(vo)* Come on uncle, show me how already!

GEORGE: *(vo)* How come I always gotta patch net?

MRS. YAMAMOTO: *(vo)* Alika, we're waiting!

ALIKA: *(sits up in bed, dresses for work. To audience.)* Aloooohaaa!

> *(waits for a response from the audience, is not satisfied, invites the audience to respond.)*

Alooohaa!

> *(audience responds)*

Mahalo, and welcome to your Aloha Tours' "Guide to O'ahu." My name is Alika and I'll be your host for today. At the helm is Big Al—best darn bus driver this side of Hollywood. This is our Historical Sights Tour and the first place we'll be going to is the Arizona Memorial. From there we'll head on over to 'Iolani Palace Grounds for lunch and end up at Punchbowl Cemetery, National Memorial of the Pacific. We at Aloha Tours are here to serve you, so if you have any questions at all, just ask! *(pause)*

So what, Al, whatchoo going do about youa girlfriend? *(nods his head, agrees with the imaginary bus driver.)*

Yeah, I tink maybe you should move in wit' her. . . . Me? Nah, I no more time. Plus, wahines . . . too much trouble—I mean for me. Eh, Al, I had one real strange dream last night. What Filipinos tink about dreams? *(laughs at Al's answer)*

No, I neva eat balut. . . . Huh? Oh, was about my cousins when we was teenagers. . . . Yeah, I know I gotta listen, but, I donno what I'm supposto hea. Ah, tanks. . . . *(nods in agreement. Turns and looks out the "window" of the bus. Addresses the audience again.)*

To your right on the hillside is the Kamehameha Schools. It was founded through the will of Princess Bernice Pauahi Bishop for the betterment of children of Hawaiian ancestry. Another ten minutes and we'll be at the Memorial.

> *(Pause. A Hawaiian woman walks to ALIKA from the audience.)*

MOM: You have a big burden to carry, but you must carry it. That's what your dreams are saying. Alika, I fed you at my breast to build your body. Who do you think feeds you your dreams? Don't hold it in like Georgie did. You need love. You need to love. Loving the dead is not enough, Alika. Your thoughts are of me and your cousin Georgie more than anyone else. You need to love life. You need to keep your aloha for life—don't lose that. Now, what about Lisa? Why can't you love her? When you first met her you hated her. Your father and I are cousins, there's nothing wrong with that. She's not even related to you. You want to love her—you just won't let yourself. I'm tired of seeing you turn love away every time it comes to you.

ALIKA: And I'm tired of losing everybody I love. Mom, please, leave me for a while. I miss you and Dad so much. But I'm working now and I can't cry in front of all these people.

MOM: Just like your father.

ALIKA: Oh, come on. Here? On the bus? Gimme a break.

MOM: You've always got an excuse—any excuse to hide.

ALIKA: Mom, why?

MOM: Why what?

ALIKA: Why everything. Why you an' Dad had to die. Why I gotta take care my cousin's daughter. Why I cannot get one good job—why everything.

MOM: You notice there's only haole birds here now?

ALIKA: What's that gotta do with anything?

MOM: Alika, you're my only bright light left. Stop drinking. It's making you so lōlō. He mau kaona kēia. I wish I had taught you so many things. But your father and I, we just let it all die with us. They made us so ashamed of who we are. E hoʻopiha i ka mākālua i hakahaka—fill the hole from which the plant has been removed.

ALIKA: What? That doesn't help me. What do you mean? Why you always talk to me in riddles?

MOM: Alika, you wouldn't know help if it bit you on the ʻōkole. Stop drinking yourself stupid. If I see you here sooner than you're supposed to be . . . oh, I'm gonna be—! Don't you dare. Do you hear me, Alika Kaleihaʻaheoʻonākūpuna Kealoha? Don't you dare! *(returns to her seat.)*

ALIKA: Mom! *(reacts to Al.)* Huh, oh, notting . . . just talking to myself. I mean I'm rehearsing a speech. . . . Jim wants to talk to me. Who knows, you know . . . everybody's been talking about da company building one moa hotel— maybe he's gonna give me a promotion now and, you know, I wanna be ready. . . .Yep, I'll take over. *(faces audience.)* And here we are at the Arizona Memorial.

SCENE 2

BOSS: *(coming out of the audience)* Alika, good afternoon. Thanks for coming by so quickly!

(They shake hands.)

Well I'll get right to the point. I called you in because we've been friends for a long time now. You've done a great job and I appreciate that. I got word today from upstairs that the corporation is expanding. We've just purchased seventy acres from a private estate, where we plan to build our next resort.

ALIKA: Wow, that's great! Congratulations!

BOSS: Thank you. I'll be taking over there as the new General Manager.

ALIKA: Wow, congratulations!

BOSS: Thank you. I'd like you to come with me and I'd like to bring you up into management.

ALIKA: Really, Jim! I mean, Mr. Mortenson.

BOSS: You can still call me Jim.

ALIKA: Jim, I really, I mean I really . . . uh, thanks. I don't know what to say.

BOSS: Well, you've worked hard for us. Clients are always coming in and telling me how gracious and helpful you are. I want to reward you for that, and, by bringing you up into management, my hope is that you'll teach that attitude to the other workers.

ALIKA: I'll give it my best shot. I promise. I'll give this company everything I got. I really want to get somewhere.

BOSS: Great, I'm glad to hear it. I knew I could count on you. One last thing, and I'm not going to mince words. The property that the corporation has purchased includes the beach where you live.

ALIKA: What!

BOSS: It came as quite a surprise to me too. For some reason I always thought your land was homestead land. I guess because I know your grandfather lived there for so many years. Don't worry, though. As soon as I heard about it, I knew I had to take care of you folks. You know the local people have always been our main concern. And that goes double for our employees. So, I talked to the board of directors personally. I told them who you are and what you do for us and they're fully prepared to help you relocate. I'll be working with the housing agency to see that everything goes as smoothly as possible. And, they're even willing to offer you a rent subsidy. Considering the shape of your grandfather's place, I think it's a big step up. Not that you haven't taken care of it. But, well, you know, it's . . . it's old. We want to break ground in two months, so you've got plenty of time to get yourself packed. Your cousin, what's his name?

ALIKA: Michael.

BOSS: Right. He can't stay on the beach. I suggest he move in with you. Now, I've let the owners know that fishing is his livelihood and I suggested to them that we pay him to show the tourists how the ancient Hawaiians used to fish. That way he can keep fishing, make some extra money, and the tourists are happy. They loved the idea. I strongly suggest that he take them up on it, or find another place to fish. There's a few more details to work out, but that's the gist of it. Okay so far?

ALIKA: What can I say?

BOSS: Alika, I hired you because you have potential. Treat this as a lesson in life. Watch what's happening and learn from it. I'm looking forward to the day when you'll be running all our tour operations. These changing times, they're for your benefit—if you know how to take advantage of them. There's money to be made. Now, as for the rent subsidy, this will come in the form of bimonthly checks—separate from your paycheck.

(ALIKA nods and smiles.)

(The BOSS returns to his seat.) These, if used for rent, will not affect your income tax status, at least we hope not. I say this because usually it would . . . but we've been speaking to our accounting department and have come up with some very clever ways. . . .

SCENE 3

(ALIKA returns home, gets undressed, drinks himself unconscious. The voices start up again.)

(Voices offstage.)

MICHAEL: *(vo)* Us guys, we stupid.

GEORGE: *(vo)* Maybe now you understand why I did what I did.

BOSS: *(vo)* Because I'm haole I can't understand?

GEORGE: *(vo)* All they do is trap you.

STEVIE: *(vo)* Ho, come on, uncle, be serious!

MICHAEL: *(vo)* Alika, 'Lika-Boy, wake up! Time fo' go schoo!

> *(MICHAEL enters, walks over to ALIKA, shakes him; they are adolescent youths once again.)*

Hurry up, we going be late.

ALIKA: Time arready, whea's Georgie?

GEORGE: *(enters carrying imaginary folders)* Right hea. Eh, let's go, Bully! We going be late!

ALIKA: Okay, okay, I coming!

MICHAEL: *(to ALIKA)* You like come wit' us fishing?

> *(ALIKA nods.)*

GEORGE: Miko, you did youa homework?

MICHAEL: No, I had fo' clean net.

GEORGE: I neva eadda.

> *(They look expectantly to ALIKA.)*

ALIKA: What if Mrs. Yamamoto fin' out?

MRS. YAMAMOTO: *(comes from audience)* Find out what, Alika?

MICHAEL: Hurry up, an' no say notting!

> *(They all jump onto bench and are at school.)*

MRS. YAMAMOTO: Alika, what was that you said?

ALIKA: Notting . . .

MRS. YAMAMOTO: Good, then you can start saying something by leading us this morning in the Pledge of Allegiance.

ALIKA: *(to MICHAEL and GEORGE)* I neva learn all da words to dat one yet!

MRS. YAMAMOTO: Alika . . . we're waiting.

ALIKA: *(comes forward)* I pledge allegiance to da flag . . . of da untidy states of America . . .

MRS. YAMAMOTO: United . . . United States of America.

ALIKA: Of da United United States of America.

(MICHAEL *and* GEORGE *giggle.*)

and to da, da . . . *(looks back to* MICHAEL *and* GEORGE *for help)*

GEORGE: *(whispering)* Republic.

MRS. YAMAMOTO: George, Alika is not going to learn if you insist on helping him.

MICHAEL: Busted!

GEORGE: Shut up!

ALIKA: An to da Freepublic . . .

(MICHAEL *and* GEORGE *laugh.*)

MICHAEL: *(to audience)* Eh, no laugh! I said you could laugh? Shut up, shut up you stupid! *(crosses to audience)*

MRS. YAMAMOTO: Michael Mahekona, come here right now! Thank you, Alika.

(MICHAEL *comes forward.*)

Now, Mr. Mahekona, apologize to the class.

MICHAEL: Sorry.

MRS. YAMAMOTO: Good. Now will you please lead us?

MICHAEL: I pledge allegiance to the flag . . . *(By the end of the pledge, he is sticking his middle finger at the teacher.)* . . . of the United States of America and to the Republic for which it stands, one nation, under God, indivisible, with liberty and justice for all.

MRS. YAMAMOTO: Thank you, Mr. Mahekona, you may now step forward.

(MICHAEL stays put.)

Step forward!

(He does.)

Put out your hand.

(He doesn't.)

Put out your hand!

(He does.)

I will not tolerate students pointing their middle finger at me.

(She slaps him hard on his open palm with a ruler. MICHAEL does not flinch.)

Now, no more of that, please. You may return to your seat.

(He does.)

Okay, now for today's lesson we will be studying verbs, adverbs, the conjugation of the aforementioned particles of speech . . .

(The three boys look at each other dumbfounded.)

. . . their specific place in the history of linguistics . . .

(The boys become hypnotized by the sound. A bell rings. They get up, gather their books, and start to go. A bell rings again and they sit.)

MRS. YAMAMOTO: Now clear your desks and take out paper and pencil. It's time for the quiz.

> *(The boys take out paper and begin to write. They start to glance slyly at each other's papers.)*

You three!

> *(They stop copying and look up at her.)*

You will not sit next to each other anymore since you can find no other way to get through school except by cheating. Move your seats please. All right, the rest of you, turn around and get back to your tests.

> *(They reluctantly sit further away from each other.)*

(She stays by ALIKA.) Alika, you boys can't keep doing each other's work—it's cheating. You have to learn to take tests on your own. I know you think I'm being mean, but I'm not. You boys are going to be tested all your lives. And you can't expect that your cousins are always going to be there to help you out. When you graduate, your cousins can't get you a job, or put food on your plate. And you won't be able to do that for them. I know it's tough, but you've got to start learning to do things for yourselves. Okay? *(looks at the other two)* Okay? *(resumes her place at the head of the class)* Now then, take your tests and pass them to the person in front of you. The bell's going to ring. Tomorrow fourth graders will begin chapter five in their workbooks, fifth graders . . .

> *(The bell rings. They get up, gather their books and start to leave. The bell rings again, they sit. Bell rings, they stand, ring, sit, ring, stand. Soon, the bell rings continuously until MICHAEL gets fed up, throws his books to the floor.)*

MICHAEL: I hate this shit!

MRS. YAMAMOTO: Michael Mahekona, to the Principal's Office! Now!

MICHAEL: Fuck you, Jap! Come on, let's get outta here.

(GEORGE throws his books down and follows MICHAEL. The teacher looks to ALIKA. He gathers his books and walks out.)

MRS. YAMAMOTO: Damn.

SCENE 4

(MICHAEL and GEORGE mime carrying fish nets.)

ALIKA: You guys finish da patching?

GEORGE: No, still get couple moa holes. *(to ALIKA)* Go get one needle.

ALIKA: *(accepts from MICHAEL a net to ptach.)* Miko, how you can tell where da āholehole goin' turn?

MICHAEL: 'Cause dey always turn da same way when da wave comes. You just gotta watch.

GEORGE: I goin' get one fat moi today.

MICHAEL: Eh, what I said? No talk about whatchoo goin' catch! Ho, you no can listen, ah?

GEORGE: 'Lika, you pau youa hole?

ALIKA: Yeah, I pau.

MICHAEL: What about you slow poke?

GEORGE: Jus' a minute, jus' a minute! At leas' my patches no break, ah?

MICHAEL: Eh, whatchoo mean, was da nylon dat wen' broke, not my patch.

ALIKA: When my net goin' be pau?

MICHAEL: Wensday.

ALIKA: How much we still owe?

GEORGE: Wait, lemme see. . . . *(takes out a crumpled piece of paper from his pocket and reads it)* We owe Mista Lee ten moa pounds.

(ALIKA looks to MICHAEL)

MICHAEL: Maybe today. Maybe. You goin' chrow, but, since it's fo' youa net.

GEORGE: Tsk! Ho, I tought was my turn?

MICHAEL: Yeah, yeah, you can chrow, but only afta 'Lika-Boy catches what he needs.

GEORGE: Ho, we goin' be dea all aftanoon. . . .

MICHAEL: Eh, you pau yet, big mout?

GEORGE: Yeah, why, you big mout! An . . . you ugly too!

MICHAEL: Yeah, I ugly, but I can catch fish, all you can catch is one cold.

(MICHAEL and GEORGE go at it, trading insults.)

ALIKA: Ho, can we go? You guys always fight too much. I tink you love each odda.

MICHAEL: Yeah, da's right, I love him—he's my brudda da's why. But he's just one punk, da's why.

GEORGE: Eh, no call me punk, ugly. You one ugly punk and you get pīlau breat!

MICHAEL: Yeah, yeah, yeah, so you love me too cuz we bruddas. Put da needles away an' shut up arready!

GEORGE: *(Mimicking MICHAEL.)* Put da needles away an' shut up arready!

MICHAEL: You know what, 'Lika, I tink you're right. He no stop talking—I tink he's one girl.

GEORGE: *(mimicking MICHAEL)* You know what 'Lika, I tink you're right. He no stop talking. I tink he's one girl.

MICHAEL: You like beef!

GEORGE: No. I like chicken!

MICHAEL: Ah come, we go arready, 'Lika. *(to GEORGE)* You giving me one headache!

GEORGE: Youa pīlau breat backing up in youa head da's why. . . .

MICHAEL: Shut up! Shut up! Shut up!

GEORGE: Oh, oh. Tree strikes, I'm out.

ALIKA: Georgie, let him go arready, you wen' win.

> *(MICHAEL and GEORGE sling the nets over their shoulders. They mime getting into a canoe and lay the nets down. ALIKA gets in also.)*

MICHAEL: Mākaukau?

ALIKA and GEORGE: 'Ae.

MICHAEL: Hoe!

> *(They begin to paddle the canoe, start a paddling chant, MICHAEL leads.)*

Hoe aku i kou wa'a
Hoe, hoe

Nānā i ka Hōkūpaʻa
Hahai i ka Hōkūleʻa
Auwē! ʻO Hawaiʻi kēia!

(GEORGE stops paddling. MICHAEL notices this.)

Eh headless, wassamatta? Youa arm broke?

GEORGE: Shut up! You headless! I get one cramp.

MICHAEL: I going give you one cramp. You pull youa own weight.

GEORGE: Okay, okay, geeze . . .

(They resume the chant. The chant ends.
MICHAEL pulls back on the steering, the other
two brace for a landing. ALIKA jumps out first,
followed by GEORGE, then MICHAEL. They
mime dragging the canoe out of the water.
They get the nets ready.)

ALIKA: I neva see da wata so mālie.

GEORGE: I did. Dat time you was sick. Lucky ting too! Oa else me
an' Miko woudda neva made it back. We had so much
fish! Yeah Miko?

MICHAEL: Oh yeah, 'memba, Georgie . . . our folks was so happy
wit da mullet they wen let us bot' get drunk!

GEORGE: Yeah, den I got sick.

MICHAEL: Well, smat-head, nobody tol' you fo' drink so much.

GEORGE: Why? You can hando?

MICHAEL: Da's right.

GEORGE: Ah, you don't know.

MICHAEL: (passes the nets to ALIKA) If you gonna chrow, you gotta
carry.

(*ALIKA instantly becomes a fisherman. The other two mimic him, crouching down, giggling at him, poking each other.*)

ALIKA: Shhhh! The fish goin' hear you!

(*MICHAEL and GEORGE try to stop giggling, quiet down for a second, then erupt into laughter again.*)

ALIKA: I neva laugh wen we was fishing fo' youa guys nets!

(*MICHAEL and GEORGE stop giggling. ALIKA goes back to watching, spots something, tenses up, readies the net, watches, then throws.*)

GEORGE: (*running up and peering in*) You missed.

MICHAEL: (*to GEORGE*) Just shut up and get da net, you lōlō. You waited too long, 'Lika. You gotta chrow jus' afta da wave breaks, den dey cannot see 'em coming.

(*ALIKA resets the net. MICHAEL and GEORGE step back. ALIKA readies himself.*)

ALIKA: Will you show me when?

MICHAEL: Yep. Get ready! . . . Ready! . . . Now!

(*ALIKA throws. They all stand and peer. MICHAEL smiles.*)

Eh, you wen get 'em! Georgie, get da line.

(*GEORGE gets down low and pulls up the imaginary line. As he pulls, the others help him. From the looks of their efforts, the weight must be heavy.*)

ALIKA: Arright! Dis is way moa den ten pounds, hah Georgie?

MICHAEL: Of coase. Who you had fo' help you, ah?

GEORGE: *(takes out a fish and holds it up)* Look at dis moi. Mus' be almos' five pounds! Try see. *(mimes throwing the fish to MICHAEL)*

ALIKA: Eh, no play wit da fish like dat. You goin' lose 'em!

MICHAEL: *(catching the fish and whistling)* No kidding. Dis one big fish. *(throws the fish back in the ocean)*

ALIKA: Whatchoo doing?

MICHAEL: 'Lika-Boy, 'memba, you always chrow da firs' one back. Oddawise, Ke Akua going be mad.

GEORGE: Still get way 'nuff fo' get youa net. Calm down.

MOM: *(stands up in audience)* So you have your own net now?

> *(GEORGE goes over and solemnly puts a "net"*
> *into ALIKA's hands.)*

Good. Now you can fish for money, Alika.

ALIKA: Whatchoo mean, Mom? We jus' got da fish.

MOM: And then you give the fish to Mister Lee and he gives you a net of your own. And then . . . *(pause)* Oh my boy, what's Mama gonna do? If I teach you to fish it won't feed you for a lifetime—we don't live in that world anymore. You need to know how to live in this world.

ALIKA: Yes, Mama.

> *(ALIKA is drawn back to his cousins. MICHAEL*
> *motions for them to spread out. They spread*
> *out, wait, then throw their nets and pull them*
> *up in unison. They repeat this several times.*
> *The mother watches.)*

MICHAEL: 'Nuff arready. Come, we go.

> *(They gather their nets, get back into the canoe*
> *and paddle home.)*

ALIKA: Georgie, sing the one, "Me ke aloha . . ."

GEORGE: *(singing)* I remember days when we were younger. We used to catch 'o'opu in the mountain streams. 'Round the Ko'olau hills we'd ride on horseback, so long ago it seems it was a dream. Last night I dreamt I was returning, and my heart called out to you. But I fear you won't be like I left you. Me ke aloha ku'u home o Kahalu'u. I remember days when we were wiser . . .

> *(MICHAEL and GEORGE fight and argue over who sings better or worse. They fall off and disappear into the shadows. ALIKA laughs at his memory then realizes he's awake—and home. He looks at his watch—he's late! He dresses hurriedly.)*

SCENE 5

(As ALIKA readies for work, voices offstage.)

MRS. YAMAMOTO: *(vo)* I know you think I'm being mean, but I'm not.

STEVIE: *(vo)* Aloha everybody.

BOSS: *(vo)* I hired you because you have potential.

LISA: *(vo)* Can you take Stevie?

STEVIE: *(vo)* Come on, uncle, show me how!

ALIKA: *(to audience)* Aloooohaaa!

> *(He waits for a response from the audience, is not satisfied and invites the audience to respond.)*

Alooohaa!

(Audience responds.)

Mahalo, and welcome to Hawaiʻi! My name is Alika, and I'll be your guide today through this land of aloha. Loading up the luggage over there is Big Al, best darn bus driver this side of Hollywood. You can go ahead an' step on the bus now. As soon as we're all packed up we'll be ready to roll. If I can help in any way to make your stay here more enjoyable, or, if you have any questions about our lovely islands, just ask. The people of Hawaiʻi are known world-wide for their graciousness and hospitality!

(MRS. CLEMENTS, sitting in the audience, raises her hand. MR. CLEMENTS, sitting next to her, tries to pull her arm back down.)

MRS. CLEMENTS: Excuse me, Mr. Alika? Henry, stop that!

MR. CLEMENTS: Hell, Mabel, we ain't even started the tour yet.

MRS. CLEMENTS: He said to ask and I have a question. *(to ALIKA)* I'm sorry, honey. He had a bit of gas on the plane so he's not in the best of moods.

MR. CLEMENTS: Mabel, you're embarrassing me!

MRS. CLEMENTS: Tit for tat . . . now what I'd like to know, Mr. Alika, if you please, is what the meaning of "aloha" is. You see we're from the South, and at home we have what we call "Southern Hospitality." But I don't believe it's the same thing as your "aloha." Now, as a teacher of American history, I've always been . . .

MR. CLEMENTS: Mabel, he don't care that you're a teacher of American history. . . .

MRS. CLEMENTS: Well, none of the stewardesses cared to see your Elvis mole, but you went ahead and shared it with them anyway. And I didn't say one word. So if you know what's best for you, you should consider hushing your mouth. My deepest apologies Mr. Alika. Again, all I wanted to know was what your understanding of "aloha" is.

ALIKA: *(to audience)* The question was, what does "aloha" mean. Well, "aloha" means many things, it can mean "hello," "farewell," "I love you"—it all depends on the situation and how you use it.

MRS. CLEMENTS: *(standing up and walking over to* ALIKA*)* Thank you, Mr. Alika. Just one more thing . . . *(takes him over to the side)* My name is Mabel Louise Clements. I'm very pleased to meet you.

> *(They shake hands.)*

ALIKA: Alika Kealoha. You can just call me Alika. Nice to meet you, ma'am.

> *(All through the scene* MR. CLEMENTS *takes pictures of them in various poses.)*

MRS. CLEMENTS: Now as I was saying, I'm an American history teacher, and it has always fascinated me that America is such a melting pot. And when I was studying in college, I found Hawayee—I hope I'm pronouncing that right—to be the most fascinating place of all because here you all are—so many different races and religions in such a small space—but you all seem to get along just fine. And the more I read, the more it seemed that you all could do this because of something called "aloha." Because you're a Hawaiian, let me ask you this . . . you see it's real important for me to understand this. As a Hawaiian, what's your understanding of "aloha?"

ALIKA: You mean as a Hawaiian?

MRS. CLEMENTS: Just as a Hawaiian man. Nothing to do with tours, or speeches. . . .

ALIKA: Well thank you for asking, ma'am. As a Hawaiian, I'd like to say that "aloha" is . . . "Aloha" . . . I donno ma'am, it's really hard to explain. It's like, it's like if you got lost here and you needed my help, then I'd take you home, feed you, offer my house to you. It's other things too, but you really have to see it.

YOUNG MALE TOURIST: *(from audience)* Hey man, where can we get, you know, lei'd?

MRS. CLEMENTS: *(ignores remark)* Thank you, Alika, thank you very much.

ALIKA: You're welcome, ma'am.

(MR. and MRS. CLEMENTS exit.)

Good question! That will take us right into our first destination, Waikīkī! As you probably noticed on your flight over, Waikīkī has become the largest, most sophisticated destination in our lovely islands. And there you'll find many hula shows and Hawaiian feasts, called lūʻaus, that you can visit. There's a reproduction of an ancient Hawaiian village, complete with grass shacks, in the Royal Hawaiian Shopping Center. Did you know that there's even talk of building a space-port on the Big Island of Hawaiʻi? Yep, we're moving into the Age of the Pacific!

(LISA enters with STEVIE. STEVIE has bandages on her arms. They wave, trying to get ALIKA's attention.)

(ALIKA notices them as he finishes his speech.)

Uh, excuse me for a second folks, the lady with the paycheck is here. What's up, Stevie?

(STEVIE holds up three fingers.)

Three shots! Boy, pretty soon they're going to have to give you a medal, ah!

LISA: *(handing him a set of keys)* Thanks for letting me use your car. I'm sorry we're so late, but her Uncle Michael didn't show up to get her. Can you take Stevie? I was afraid we were gonna miss you.

ALIKA: No problem, I only got one more stop. How'd it go?

LISA: She's okay now. The asthma was in a cycle and to break it they had to give her three. But she's okay. . . .

ALIKA: Great!

LISA: Alika, the doctor said it would be best if we stayed at your place as often as we can because the air out there is better for her. I mean, we're over there all the time anyway. . . .

ALIKA: Yeah, sure, no problem. So what, Stevie, one ice cream on da way home?

STEVIE: Ummm, yeah!

LISA: Stevie, what did the doctor say?

STEVIE: He said I can't have anything with milk in it.

ALIKA: Ahhh, what, now you cannot even eat ice cream! Jus' go buy one baby scoop. Dis'll be da lass.

LISA: Alika, please don't. She has to learn now or she'll never get better.

ALIKA: What, one scoop! It's not gonna kill her!

LISA: Alika.

ALIKA: Yeah, okay. Sorry, girl.

STEVIE: We can go fishing tomorrow wit' Uncle Miko?

ALIKA: Maybe. We gotta go already. See you back at the house.

LISA: Yea, I have to get to work too. Be good now. Both of you. *(exits)*

ALIKA: Thanks for waiting everyone! Let's go, Al. I would like to introduce all of you to my niece, Stevie. Say aloha to everyone.

STEVIE: Aloha everyone.

ALIKA: Okay, before we hit Waikīkī, we're going to take you wonderful folks past some places of interest on the island—kinda let you get a feel for things so you can decide what tours you wanna take next. A highlight we have on our tours is a visit to Punchbowl Cemetery, the National Memorial of the Pacific. That's where all the brave soldiers who fought for America's freedom rest in peace. From there we'll travel through downtown Honolulu. May I suggest a meal sometime at one of Chinatown's famous restaurants. ʻIolani Palace sits right on the outskirts of downtown. It's the only royal palace within the boundaries of the U.S. In 1893, Queen Liliʻuokalani, the last reigning monarch of Hawaiʻi, gave up her throne to become part of the United States. First, a Provisional Government was set up to convince Congress that we were really ready to be a state. Then in 1898 we became an official Territory and in 1959 we were finally admitted as the Fiftieth State.

(GEORGE enters and startles ALIKA.)

GEORGE: Nah, cuz, cherry. Erreytings rad.

ALIKA: Directly makai, that means toward the ocean, we'll see the famous statue of King Kamehameha the First—unifier of the Hawaiian Islands.

GEORGE: Nah, no worry. I goin' tell Miko we go learn deep-sea fishing. Eh, we can bring in big bucks!

ALIKA: Before Kamehameha, most of Hawaiʻi was ruled by feudal chiefs in constant battle with each other for dominance over the islands. With the help of American merchants

. . . Here we are everyone—see you all later . . . . *(Pause. Puts STEVIE down. They are back home.)*

GEORGE: You know how much 'ahi's goin' for now. Unreal. So what, we goin' smoke tonight? I heard Randall get some good buds.

ALIKA: Stevie go play outside. Uncle is busy.

STEVIE: Fine then. *(exits)*

ALIKA: Den whatchoo goin' do?

GEORGE: Oh, I donno, probly go eat, ah. Afta we smoke goin' get munchies, ah?

ALIKA: No, I mean about Lisa.

GEORGE: Oh, when I get 'nuff money, she goin' get one abortion. Stay legal now.

ALIKA: It's too late.

GEORGE: What? Dey wen change da laws again?

ALIKA: No, it's too late for her. She's six months arready. She cannot get one.

GEORGE: Dat frickin' bitch! Da's why she left me, ah?

ALIKA: Georgie, you cannot make her do what she no like do.

GEORGE: Eh, cuz, you too much! She tells me she's hāpai, den next ting I know I cannot fin' her. So I figga, arright, she wen get one abortion on her own. I goin' pay her back an' take care her when she comes back. Now she's back an' she tells me she goin' have da kid an' if I like marry her. Da's fuckin' bullshit.

ALIKA: I know. But cannot do notting. Now we gotta tink of da baby.

GEORGE: Baby? What baby? I don't see no baby. She goin' get one abortion.

ALIKA: I tol' you, cannot arready. Georgie, listen, she's goin' for have da baby an' you goin' be da fadda. Besides, what da baby wen' do? Da baby neva lie, it neva hurt nobody. An' it needs one fadda.

GEORGE: Eh, you know what, 'Lika-Boy, what da fuck you know? Hah? Whatchoo fuckin' know. You neva even had one girl yet, you stay cherry! An' you like tell me what fo' do wit one chick? Eh, fuck you brah. You wait, you goin' see, all dey do is trap you.

ALIKA: I know, but da baby . . .

(STEVIE enters.)

GEORGE: Eh, cuz, you too much! Whose fuckin' side you on anyway? She's jus' one fuckin' haole bitch. An' if she no like get one abortion, I goin' straighten her out—

ALIKA: Georgie, you're not listening. I'm just trying to—

GEORGE: Fuck you!

STEVIE: Is something wrong, Uncle?

ALIKA: No, nothing.

(LISA enters.)

LISA: I'm home.

STEVIE: Mom! *(runs to LISA)* How're you doing, Mommy? Sit down. Lemme take your bag. Is there anything I can get you? Do you wanna read the paper?

LISA: Stevie, leave Mom alone. Gimme a chance to sit down first.

ALIKA: 'As arright, Stevie, go get Uncle one beer.

STEVIE: Okay.

LISA: Thanks, Alika.

STEVIE: *(stares at LISA. Pause.)* Now? How's about fishing with Uncle Michael?

LISA: Well, I donno, have you finished all your homework?

STEVIE: Well, you see Mom, it's like this . . .

LISA: Here it comes.

STEVIE: Mom, I'm being serious.

LISA: Right.

STEVIE: You see, Mommy, there are certain, how should we say, peak studying times.

LISA: Uh, huh.

STEVIE: And, scientific evidence has shown that for fifth graders, because of the junk television on Sunday nights, that's the best time for studying.

ALIKA: Is that your best shot?

(BUILDING INSPECTOR knocks.)

Hello?

INSPECTOR: Hello. Um, I'm the building inspector from Paradise Industrials. I was told you'd be expecting me about six-thirty. I just need to make some preliminary inspections. It'll only take a few minutes.

ALIKA: *(under his breath)* Shit. *(to the INSPECTOR)* Uh, yeah, just a minute.

LISA: Alika, what's this about?

ALIKA: I'll tell you later. *(to the INSPECTOR)* Come inside.

INSPECTOR: Thanks, it should only take a couple of minutes. They told you I was coming, didn't they?

ALIKA: No.

INSPECTOR: Oh, I'm sorry. They told me they scheduled it with you for six-thirty. You know what? I feel bad, I'll come back another time.

ALIKA: No, no, you're here already. Why don't you just do it.

INSPECTOR: You sure?

ALIKA: Yep. This my niece, Stevie, and her mother, Lisa.

LISA: Hi.

STEVIE: Hello.

INSPECTOR: Hi. Sorry to interrupt you folks, I'll just be a few minutes.

ALIKA: You want a beer?

INSPECTOR: Oh, no thank you. I'm still on the job. I just came to check out your plumbing and electricity. I can take a look around?

ALIKA: Yep. The bathroom's over there.

> (STEVIE *follows the* INSPECTOR *around the house.*)

INSPECTOR: How long have you folks lived here?

ALIKA: I don't know when my grandfadda moved in. But I tink he had it for a long time befoa I was born. He used to work on the plantation. We've been here ever since I was about twelve, maybe.

INSPECTOR: Oh. I was just asking 'cause nobody has any records of this place. You did those patches in the bathroom yourself?

ALIKA: Yeah, I did it a coupla years ago. Is there a problem?

INSPECTOR: No, no, no. It's a real good job. You one plumba?

ALIKA: No. My Tūtū man was a . . . well, he was a craftsman and he taught us to take care of stuff ourselves. *(ALIKA pulls STEVIE away from the INSPECTOR.)*

INSPECTOR: Yeah, old people, they're smart, ah? My grandfather was like that too. Chee, I wish I paid more attention to him—he knew plenny, that guy.

ALIKA: Yeah, I wish mine was here for Stevie.

INSPECTOR: No additions to these pipes? And, one main line here . . . well, I got all I need. *(starts to leave.)* Eh, sorry they neva tell you I was coming by. Sometimes I don't like the way they do things, you know.

> *(ALIKA nods.)*

My parents, they used to have a house just like this in Kalihi. Plenny memories, yeah? Solid, these houses. Ah, sorry. I'm going. Good night.

ALIKA: Night.

INSPECTOR: Good night.

LISA: Bye.

STEVIE: Good night.

LISA: Alika, I was going to cook some stew for dinner. You want some? Alika . . .

> *(silence)*

Stevie, cook some rice.

> *(STEVIE exits.)*

> *(ALIKA, MICHAEL, GEORGE, and LISA are shopping for a boat. They mime checking them out.)*

GEORGE: I always wanted one Radden motor boat.

MICHAEL: Maybe we should get one deep-well boat, go learn deep-sea fishing, too.

GEORGE: Nah, we stick to what we know. We go get one Radden can take us aroun', we go lay lobsta net, fish net, dive. We goin' make plenny money. Ho, you seen how much lobsta cos' in da stoa, hah, 'Lika-Boy?

ALIKA: I donno. We neva run one business befo'. Maybe we should talk to somebody.

MICHAEL: Whatchoo mean, we been selling fish from small kid time. But now, when we get one boat, we can hit all da choice spots. You goin' graduate one moa yea. I like take care you. By dat time we going be jammin! Dat boat goin' be custom out! We goin' be selling Tamashiro Market 'stead of Mista Lee.

GEORGE: Check dis moto out! Heavy ah. Radical. Dis baby can fly.

MICHAEL: You seen dis one? One Volvo Penta Inboad Tree Tousand–frickin' bitchin'!

GEORGE: We going sell Farma's Market too! We going walk inside da market, dey goin' beg fo' us give dem fish. *(to LISA)* Hah, Honey?

(LISA smiles.)

You know it! Da Tree Muskateers of da Ocean! Brudda Brudda Captain Miko at da wheel!

MICHAEL: *(climbs into the boat and takes the wheel)* Brudda Brudda "Squid Eye" Georgie-Boy hanging off da side, searchin' fo' da he'e. An' Brudda Brudda 'Lika-Boy . . . patching net.

ALIKA: Ah, what, I always gotta patch net!

MICHAEL: Nah, nah, nah, nah, I just kidding—I couldn't tink of anyting rhyme whichyoua name. Sorry, ah.

GEORGE: *(to LISA)* I going tell 'em, kay Honey?

(LISA smiles.)

When everyting works out wit da fishing, den me an' Lisa going get married an', you know—get one family.

MICHAEL: Eh, right on, cuz! Congrats! Lisa, you're one good girl. You stick by Georgie-Boy. You good cook too. Chee, I donno what fo' say. I sounding kinda stupid I guess, ah? Congratulations.

LISA: Well, we haven't planned anything yet. We're really just talking about it.

MICHAEL: 'Lika-Boy, you not goin' say notting?

ALIKA: I tink we . . . I mean . . . ho, why you guys make me say dis.

MICHAEL: Say what? All you gotta say is congratulations. It's not like you gotta say da Pledge of Allegiance, ah?

ALIKA: Yeah, funny.

MICHAEL: Well, what you got fo' say?

GEORGE: 'Lika-Boy, what's wrong?

ALIKA: You know my Mom wanted you guys fo' go back schoo.

MICHAEL: What dat gotta do wit Georgie getting married?

ALIKA: Da's not what I'm talking about. You know what I mean. We wen talk about dis befo' she wen pass away. She wanted us all fo' go school. Da insurance money is for me go college an' you guys go one trade school. Why you make me say this in front Lisa.

MICHAEL: You tink you feel bad. How you tink we wen' feel when Aunty tol' us go back schoo'? She knows we bot' hate schoo', but she like make us promise we going go. You tink it's easy fo' us break Aunty's promise? Hah? Georgie-

Boy an' me wen' talk long time. We jus' goin' waste
Aunty's money if we go school. Cuz, us guys, we stupid.
We not like you. We neva go private school. We was
hoping you would use youa brains fo' help us out. Alika,
I know youa mudda wanted for us get ahead, but, we jus'
fishamen. We happy wen we fishing. Hah, Georgie?

(GEORGE *nods.*)

What's wrong wit' dat? Why we gotta do more?

GEORGE: Long time, you know, we wen' wait fo' you come back
fish wit' us. We was waiting all dese yeas. 'Lika-Boy, you
happy going schoo'? You like go four more years?
Everytime you get one vacation, bam, you out wit us. I
telling you 'Lika-Boy, dey selling you all da wrong stuff.
Come on, cuz.

ALIKA: I donno. I gotta tink.

MICHAEL: Whatchoo like tink about? Hah? How much furdda
away from us you like get? What, maybe you jus' shame
us da's why? Hah? What, you like go college, go learn
moa den youa stupid cousins, ah? What Kam Schoo' wen
teach you? Dat youa cousins, we some stupid mokes?
Hah? I tell you someting. Bot us guys, we knew betta.
When we went take da tes', we wen' jus' act stupid. Da's
right—'cause we knew dey jus' wanted fo' teach us how
be haoles.

ALIKA: Den why you guys wen back me up when I wanted fo' go!
Why you neva tell me? I taughtchoo wanted me fo' go.

MICHAEL: 'Lika, afta youa fadda wen die, youa mudda, she had
hard time. Youa mudda, she knew she was goin' die long
befo' she tol' you. She made me an' Georgie swear dat we
would see you chru high schoo'. I tol' her, Aunty, 'Lika-
Boy, he was boan like us, in da ocean. Us, we get salt
wata in ouwa veins. 'Lika-Boy, us Hawaiians, we been
fishing in deese watas fo' how many centries. All youa

kupunas, all da people dat made you, dey all lived and breed chru da ocean. We came hea on da ocean. When you in da ocean, you wit' youa 'ohana. Whea we get ouwa food from? An' ouwa parents—how dey wen feed demselves? And ouwa parents' parents? An' all ouwa 'ohana right down da mo'o's back from when da mo'o firs' when climb onto da lan'. An' all dose Hawaiians up at Kam Schoo', I love 'um, dey's all my bruddas, but dey like us foget who we are. An' college, foget it, dey no even want us dea.

ALIKA: Ah, I'm so mix up arreday. Why Mama neva tell me notting?

MICHAEL: Alika, what she goin' tell you? You goin' lose bot' youa parents? Shit, I no like talk arreday. I shoulda neva tol' you. We jus' like take care you, boy.

ALIKA: . . . One Radden sounds good. . . . I tired us paddle canoe.

MICHAEL: Da's my boy. (*pats ALIKA on the shoulder*) We going be arright.

(*ALIKA is left alone. He falls asleep.*)

SCENE 6

(*Next morning. ALIKA asleep on the beach, curled up where he stood. MOM and LISA come to ALIKA's side and gently wake him.*)

MOM: You see these pebbles . . .

LISA: Alika.

ALIKA: Yes, Mama?

LISA: Alika, it's me, Lisa.

ALIKA: *(wakes up, startled)* Huh? Oh. What time is it?

LISA: Seven-thirty. Stevie's still asleep.

ALIKA: Tanks, I'll be up in a minute.

LISA: You wanna talk?

> *(ALIKA shakes his head.)*

I'm here if you wanna talk.

> *(ALIKA nods. As she goes back to the house he stretches out.)*

MOM: There, there, what was that?

ALIKA: What was what?

MOM: That. She comes down, shows she cares, wants to help. What do you do? Give her the cold shoulder.

ALIKA: What was I supposed to do? Take her in my arms and kiss her? I got halitosis.

MOM: That's not what I meant. You could have talked about your problems. Instead you make her feel unwanted. But I didn't say anything about kissing—that was your idea. Are you saying that all you need is a little toothpaste to help you out?

ALIKA: No, I'm not saying that's what I need. I don't want that and I don't want her to get the wrong idea. Mom, I know Lisa cares for me. I know she loves me. But I don't love her that way and I don't want her to get the wrong idea.

MOM: What idea, that she's allowed in the same universe?

ALIKA: You know what I mean.

MOM: *(pause)* You see these pebbles . . .

ALIKA: Mom, I don't need you to tell me about rocks. I need you here.

MOM: You don't know what you need, Alika. That's the problem. All I have is my stories. You will listen to them.

ALIKA: I've been listening to people all my life. It's time I did something for myself.

MOM: Yes it is. But you'll make your decisions by what you've learned, and if you have learned to think for yourself, then thank goodness you've finally started paying attention. Now, about these pebbles . . . Sit.

(ALIKA grabs a bottle and sits.)

My tūtū told me this story when I was very young. These pebbles, they're called 'ili'ili. Long, long ago, they were the mountains. They came up out of the ocean, they made this 'āina. The rains came down and the land grew out of this rock. The growth split the rock. They became nā pōhaku; stones and boulders. The rains continue, life grows from life and the rocks are split again and again. Now they are 'ili'ili, pebbles, and they come tumbling down the mountain and sit at the shore. And now the waves crash over them, waves from all over the world. And do you know what they do?

ALIKA: They become sand?

MOM: Very funny, but no. Sand comes from the uhu chewing up the coral. Now don't ruin your tūtū's story. The 'ili'ili try for the rest of eternity to ne'ene'e a pili, to get closer and closer to each other, trying to become that mountain again. The waves crash and crash, but the 'ili'ili, they don't separate. They tumble over each other, they smash into each other, but they keep together. Now do you understand what Tūtū was trying to say?

ALIKA: That we've been ground down to pebbles but we have to stick together.

MOM: Deeper, Alika, reach into who we are and what this life means.

ALIKA: I don't know, Mom. I don't know.

MOM: And you won't find the answer at the bottom of a bottle. *(returns to seat)*

(ALIKA sits and stares out into the ocean.)

SCENE 7

(ALIKA sits, drinking a beer. MICHAEL is teaching STEVIE how to throw net.)

MICHAEL: 'Kay now, grab all da weights togedda.

(STEVIE does so, looking for approval from MICHAEL.)

Yeah, da's it. Now lif' 'em on youa shoulda. Okay, now watch. Right afta da wave breaks, den look fo' 'em, okay?

STEVIE: Okay. *(shifts weight and crouches, reminiscent of ALIKA earlier)*

ALIKA: Wait, wait, wait, you gotta have da hat!

MICHAEL: *(puts it on STEVIE)* Eh, now da's what I call a fishaman! Okay, let's go! *(crouches behind STEVIE)*

STEVIE: Finally!

MICHAEL: Okay, now, watch da wave—

ALIKA: Wait, wait, wait!

STEVIE: Ho, now what, Uncle!

ALIKA: We neva bless da net!

STEVIE: What?

MICHAEL: Oh, yeah, yeah, I almos' forgot. Tank you brudda 'Lika-Boy.

ALIKA: Wait, Stevie. *(crosses to STEVIE)* You not goin' catch fish if you no bless da net. Now everybody, bow youa heads. Close youa eyes. God bless *(pours his beer over STEVIE)* dis lōlō head girl.

STEVIE: That's not funny.

ALIKA: Well hmmm, hmmm, hmmm, you goin' be one nuha girl now?

(STEVIE chases them.)

MICHAEL: Wassa matta, girl? You goin' get wet anyway.

SECURITY GUARD: *(enters)* Howsit.

MICHAEL: Howsit, wass up.

ALIKA: What's up. *(hides his beer)*

GUARD : Any luck yet?

MICHAEL: Nah, we jus' teaching da girl how fo' chrow.

SECURITY GUARD : Well, good luck.

MICHAEL: Yeah, tanks.

(The GUARD exits.)

'Lika, wassa security guard doin' down hea?

ALIKA: Oh, I donno, maybe, uh, he saw me drinking.

MICHAEL: No, no. I mean what is he doing down hea in da firs' place? How come he's on dis beach? Nobody comes hea but us.

STEVIE: Come on, Uncle, show me how arready. *(grabs MICHAEL and pulls him)*

MICHAEL: Yeah, yeah, okay, I'm coming.

(MICHAEL and STEVIE resume their positions.)

So, whatchu tink, 'Lika? How come get one security guard down hea?

ALIKA: Maybe he jus' came from work an' like check out da watta.

MICHAEL: Oh, well, dat makes sense. I guess soona or lata every place goin' get peopo, ah. I guess we can share da place wit some moa fishamen. I wonda if he get nets, maybe he like lay wit me?

STEVIE: Come on Uncle, you not watching.

MICHAEL: Oh, yeah, sorry ah! Gotta watch. Okay, okay, ready . . . ready . . . ready . . . ready ready . . . ready . . . ready . . . ready *(strings STEVIE out, making her wait forever)*

STEVIE: Ho, come on. Be serious!

MICHAEL: Okay, okay, serious kine! Get ready. On tree, okay?

STEVIE: Okay.

MICHAEL: One . . . two . . . tree! Chrow!

(MICHAEL grabs the back of the net and STEVIE goes sailing into the water.)

STEVIE: That wasn't funny.

MICHAEL: Oh, kulikuli, you gotta learn how fo' play.

(SECURITY GUARD enters.)

Eh, howsit brudda. So what, you fish?

SECURITY GUARD: I'm afraid you folks gotta leave.

MICHAEL: What? Yeah, right. No, serious kine, you get nets, or poles, or you one diva?

SECURITY GUARD: I'm really sorry, but you're all going to have to leave.

MICHAEL: Eh, brudda, no fool around. I don't know you dat well yet.

SECURITY GUARD: Look, I'm sorry, but the owners have asked that we keep the property clear.

MICHAEL: What? Ownas? Who da fuck you?

SECURITY GUARD: This property's been sold and the developers want to keep everybody off because of the liability. And especially, they don't want any illegal activities going on.

MICHAEL: Since when is fishing illegal?

SECURITY GUARD: Drinking alcoholic beverages is prohibited.

ALIKA: Yeah, yeah, okay, sorry. Uh, wait, I'll go. I'm the only one who was drinking. *(gets up to pack)*

SECURITY GUARD: I'm really sorry but the management would like you all to leave.

MICHAEL: Management, I don't see no management hea. I jus' see one stupid, fagget haole who's gonna get his face bus' up real soon.

SECURITY GUARD: Haole!

STEVIE: Uncle, just take me home.

MICHAEL: Shutchua mout'.

SECURITY GUARD: Eh, I get Hawaiian blood just like you.

MICHAEL: So whatchoo doing trying fo' kick us off ouwa beach?

SECURITY GUARD: I'm doing my job, brudda. 'Cause I get one family to feed too.

MICHAEL: Well fuck youa job! Dis is ouwa beach. We been hea since we was boan. We ain't even boddering nobody. Dea ain't even anyone else aroun'! Ah, you stay kidding, ah! What, Wally wen send you down hea? Dat frickin' guy, he catch me all da time! Whea he stay. Arright, Wally—Ha, ha, Candid Camera—you Mista Funt. You wen' get me good, whea you stay?

SECURITY GUARD: It's not a joke. If you don't vacate the premises now, I have to call the police.

MICHAEL: So you say you one Hawaiian? Den whatchoo doin? You no fish, hah? You no drink? *(moves to GUARD)*

ALIKA: *(intercedes)* Come on, Miko, cool down. We go arready.

MICHAEL: No, no, no, no, no. Dis guy, he says he's one Hawaiian. So I like know, Bully, what makes you Hawaiian?

SECURITY GUARD: 'O ko'u na'au, ko'u 'ohana a me ka 'ōlelo Hawai'i. 'Ae, 'ōlelo au i ka 'ōlelo makuahine. A 'o 'oe?

(MICHAEL cannot answer. He turns away and starts to go. The others follow.)

MICHAEL: Fuck!

SECURITY GUARD: Tsā, he pelapela wale nō. *(exits)*

(MICHAEL is on the floor, mending the nets. STEVIE is sleeping on the pūne'e. ALIKA keeps glancing over his shoulder at MICHAEL.)

ALIKA: Miko.

MICHAEL: What.

ALIKA: I gotta talk wit' you.

MICHAEL: What.

ALIKA: I know why da security guard was down at da beach.

MICHAEL: What! You wen' lie to me!

ALIKA: Miko, I had to getchoo outta dea befo' you wen' beef. I was worried about Stevie. . . .

MICHAEL: Yeah, so, what? We home now. Why he was down dea?

ALIKA: Miko, no wake up Stevie.

MICHAEL: So why he stay down dea? Spit it out arready, I ain't got all night.

ALIKA: 'Cause my company wen' buy dis land an' dey going build one moa hotel ova hea.

MICHAEL: What! Youa company!

ALIKA: Shhh, Miko, Stevie!

MICHAEL: Eh, Stevie, wake up! Stevie Kalei!

(STEVIE gets up.)

Dea, now she's up. Now you tell me what dis bullshit is all about.

ALIKA: Miko, calm down, it's not as bad as it sounds.

MICHAEL: What? Ah, come on, 'Lika-Boy, no fuck around wit' me. How long we been hea!

ALIKA: I know, jus' listen.

MICHAEL: An' whose house is dis?

ALIKA: I know, I know, wait!

MICHAEL: How can dey buy da lan', I taut da Chong family wen' own dis lan'?

ALIKA: Dey sold it, I guess.

MICHAEL: So how come dey neva tell us?

ALIKA: Ouwa lease ran out a coupla' yeas ago. I neva had da money to get annoda one—we arready went put everyting into da boat. Dey said as long as I keep da place clean an' quiet dey not goin' bodda. But dey said dey was goin' fo' try an' sell da place. I guess I neva see anyting happening fo' long time, so I tought maybe dey would jus' forget about dis' place.

MICHAEL: Yeah, right. Somebody gonna foget about land in Hawai'i. How come you neva tell me notting?

ALIKA: What I going say? Sell da boat? I tol' you in high schoo' we shoulda neva bought dat boat. You an Georgie was da bes' fishamen I know.

MICHAEL: No talk about Georgie.

ALIKA: You guys was da bes' fishamen aroun'.

MICHAEL: I said no talk about Georgie!

ALIKA: But you neva know how fo' run one business. You everytime giving da fish away. Yeah, you guys had plenny friends, but da bank, dey neva take fish.

MICHAEL: So what you saying, I loss da boat, hah? Was my fault? An' Georgie, he's my fault too? Hah, is dat whatchoo saying!

ALIKA: Miko, stop it arready.

MICHAEL: You, you was da smat one. You was supposed to help us out!

ALIKA: Come on, Miko, I only went high school. How you expect me fo' know what to do?

MICHAEL: Waste time you went Kam anyway, dey neva teach you notting!

ALIKA: What! You so frickin' mix up! You neva like me go dea in da firs' place 'cause dey was going teach me all da haole ways. An' now dat you find out I neva wen' listen, you mad at dem fo' not teaching me da haole ways.

MICHAEL: You was supposed to learn dea game so we could beat 'em!

ALIKA: Miko, I neva sell ouwa place, whatchoo yelling at me for?

MICHAEL: It's youa company.

ALIKA: Oh yeah, right. Like I own 'em. Even if I neva work fo' da company, dey still woudda bought da lan'—at leas' dis way dey know we stay hea. My boss said dey goin' help us out.

MICHAEL: Oh, yeah? What dey goin' do? Make us one touris' attraction? Hah? You goin' bring 'em on youa tours down hea? *(imitating ALIKA)* "Here we are folks, here's a poor Hawaiian family doing some traditional Hawaiian fishing!" So what, cuz, whatchua friends goin' do fo' us poor Hawaiians?

ALIKA: Dey goin' give us one place in town fo' live.

MICHAEL: I ain't goin live in one frickin' rat hole in town. If I wanted fo' live in one house, I woulda live hea all dis time. I live on da beach, an' das whea I goin' stay.

ALIKA: If you live in town wit me, den dey said you can keep on fishing hea.

MICHAEL: Yeah, right. With a hundred touris' watching me, how I goin' catch anyting?

ALIKA: They said they'll pay you to teach the tourists how to fish.

MICHAEL: 'Lika-Boy? 'Lika-Boy, look at me. No tell me you wen' take dat from youa boss.

ALIKA: What I goin' do, what I goin' say? I gotta pay da bills. I gotta help take care Stevie. We cannot jus' eat fish.

MICHAEL: 'Lika-Boy, how you can do dis to me.

ALIKA: What I suppose to do, cuz? I no like you stop fishing. An' we cannot stop dem. You cannot fight 'em.

MICHAEL: So you wen' sell me, hah? You wen' sell youa cousin like I was one fuckin' sideshow? Whatchoo going do next, pimp Lisa out? I been taking care you since you was boan!

ALIKA: Miko, I donno what fo' do! I'm jus' trying fo' . . .

MICHAEL: Fuck you! *(exits)*

> *(Pause. ALIKA gets a beer. Notices STEVIE is up.)*

ALIKA: *(to STEVIE)* Go sleep, it'll be arright.

STEVIE: Uncle, I'm sorry.

ALIKA: Stevie, just go sleep, please.

STEVIE: Yes, Uncle. *(Turns over and goes back to sleep.)*

> *(Pause. ALIKA goes over and sits next to her.
> Rubs STEVIE's back and drinks his beer.
> GEORGE enters.)*

GEORGE: She's so beautiful. Lucky she looks like her Mom. You unnastan' now, maybe, why I did what I did? Come on, cuz, talk to me please? Lonely out hea. Everytime she smiles, hurts me so bad.

ALIKA: What happened to you, you neva say one word to us. Everytime we talked, you was jus' joking, laughing. You neva tell us notting was wrong.

GEORGE: 'Cause I was shame. I was shame I neva have money. When Lisa got pregnant she started talking 'bout all da tings she wanted fo' da baby, fo' da marriage. I know she neva mean fo' hurt me, but, I felt so bad 'cause I knew we neva was goin' have 'nuff money an' no way I was goin' put us on welfare. She wanted one special crib, she wanted all kine matching clothes fo' da baby. An fo' da marriage, she kept talking 'bout having one nice dress an' me wearing one tux.

ALIKA: So how come you neva ask us fo' help? We wouldda helped you.

GEORGE: How I goin' ask you guys fo' money? Arready we was having trouble wit' da boat. When da engine needed repairs, what, we neva have money fo' fix 'em 'cause I spent all ouwa money buying fancy reels, putting one stereo on da boat—I was so stupid.

ALIKA: We all wanted dat stuff, we was all stupid. Georgie, all I wanna know is why you neva talk wit' us? We youa bruddas. Why you wen' kill yoaself. Hah, Georgie-Boy? Why you went hang youaself! Why you left me fo' take care youa kid!

GEORGE: 'Lika-Boy, sometimes in life you get desprit. I'm sorry. But, 'Lika-Boy, I was going crazy. I couldn't stop tinking 'bout da kid. Always. How I goin' feed us, how I goin' take care her. Den I started dreaming about her. Den she started talking to me. She wasn't even boan yet an' she was talking to me!

STEVIE: *(to ALIKA)* How you goin' feed me Daddy? You no even make enough to feed yourself.

> *(The other cast members, from the wings, echo her lines and taunt GEORGE.)*

GEORGE: Stop it. I'll work it out.

STEVIE: Where we goin' live? We cannot all stay wit Alika. And what about school? Whea I goin' go?

GEORGE: Shut up arready!

STEVIE: What kinda daddy are you? You cannot even take care youaself. You smoke, you drink, you fight. . . .

GEORGE: Shut up!

STEVIE: How you goin' feed me Daddy, you cannot even feed youself. You not goin' be anyting in youa life. You don't know how fo' do notting 'cept grow pakalōlō.

GEORGE: Leave me alone!

(LISA enters.)

STEVIE: You're jus' one stupid moke.

GEORGE: Leave me alone!

LISA: George, what's wrong!

STEVIE: You're notting. An' now you like me be poor an' stupid too!

GEORGE: *(slams LISA in the stomach)* Leave me alone! I hate you! Shut up an' leave me alone!

(LISA doubles over.)

ALIKA: Georgie-Boy, Georgie, why you neva' come to us?

GEORGE: *(mimes taking a rope and making a noose)* I tried fo' kill my baby. What did I do? My baby girl. You neva do notting, you neva wen' hurt nobody. Dat was my daughter in her 'ōpū—an I wanted fo' kill her. *(puts the noose around neck)* What kind man am I? Trying fo' kill my baby. I'm sorry. *(yanks the rope and freezes)*

ALIKA: No! No. *(takes the rope off GEORGE's neck and brings him down)* Oh Georgie, Georgie, I unnastan'. *(holds GEORGE)* When I'm at work, I tink about how I goin take care her, how I goin' pay fo' her docta bills. Now she should stay hea and what, we gotta leave. What I goin' do, huh? What? I read da pepa every day, looking for one way out. I can't do dis fo' da res' of my life. I hate it. I hate da lies I havta tell. I hate da smell of coconut oil and all da burned skin. I hate da cheap plastic leis, and da stupid assholes calling me one Indian and wanting fo' take my pitcha. An' all I got is one dead cousin who leaves me take care his sick kid and one bottle beer. *(takes a swig from the beer sitting near him)*

> *(LISA enters. Listens.)*

An' you know why I drink so much? Hah, Georgie-Boy? 'Cause I can't shut those voices up. 'Cause in da back of my mind, you know, dat place whea you don't tink, you jus' feel—in da back dea I know dat dis is my rope an' if I keep drinking enough den soon I goin' . . .

LISA: Alika, what's the matter? Who are you talking to? What were you doing?

ALIKA: Burying my cousin.

LISA: What? What are you talking about? Alika, you've been drinking too much again.

ALIKA: Too much? Too much or not enough, dat is da question.

LISA: Alika, come inside.

ALIKA: Leave me alone.

<u>SCENE 8</u>

> *(LISA and STEVIE are asleep on the pūne'e.
> ALIKA comes over to watch them.)*

MOM: Now what?

> *(ALIKA shrugs his shoulders.)*

You must be thinking of something. *(pause)* Alika, they're giving you a promotion; you'll get a raise too. It's a start. You heard it yourself, he believes in you and wants to see you get ahead.

ALIKA: You jus' don't get it, Mom, I don't wanna be a tour guide. And I definitely don't wanna be one tour guide manager.

MOM: Really? That's not what you told your boss. You were pretty happy until he told you what else would happen. What if it was somebody else's land they bought? What if it was another Hawaiian family losing their land for your job? What are you standing for, Alika? Who are you angry at?

ALIKA: You just don't understand.

MOM: No, my boy, you just don't understand. America's been doing this to our people for how many years now. You've just ignored it because it hasn't hit home. Well now it has. And now you want to become Mister Activist? It's not that simple. Michael don't like America—and he don't take any of the benefits that come from it. Simple. He knows why he's angry and he knows who he hates. But not too many Hawaiians can live like that nowadays.

ALIKA: So whatchoo saying? Take da job? Shut up and move out of the only place I have left? Sell out my cousin, my brudda, my 'ohana? Huh? Is dat what you like me do?

MOM: You don't have another job waiting for you. You have a sickly niece who needs you, a woman with no one but her daughter, and a cousin so full of anger an' hurt it's just a matter of time. It's about responsibility. E kāmau 'oe. Pono 'oe e ho'okāmau. You have to carry the burden, and to do that you have to keep your aloha for life. I know it sounds stupid, our aloha's been sold and used, but for us Hawaiians it's all we got.

ALIKA: Aloha? Is that all you gotta give me!

(LISA wakes.)

LISA: What's the matter?

ALIKA: Nothing. I'm jus' talking to myself—sorry.

LISA: Are you feeling any better?

(ALIKA shrugs his shoulders.)

LISA: *(sits and watches him work)* It's gonna be a beautiful day. *(pause)* Alika . . .

ALIKA: Sixty days.

LISA: What?

ALIKA: You wanna know what's goin on, right? Well hea it is. Ouwa lease ran out a coupla yeas' ago. Da ownas jus' sol dis property—all of it—to da company dat owns my company an' dis place is goin' be one hotel.

LISA: Oh Alika . . .

ALIKA: Das' not all. My boss is going run dis new hotel, he wants me to be one of da tour managers, and we get sixty days fo' move out.

LISA: I'm sorry, I know how much this place means to you.

ALIKA: Sixty days . . . You know, as shitty as my life's been, living hea always kept me going. I could get away. I could get in da ocean. I could find peace. You know what its like fo' lose youaself in da ocean? When its so clean an' crystal clea' you can see God breathing. . . . All da fish, jus', jus' so dripping wit colors, wit life. An' all dat life around you don't know an' don't care dat you no can make rent, dat you get pukapuka pants, dat youa dad comes home drunk an' bus' up all da time, dat you mudda's got bress cancer. All dat life, jus' goin' on. When I'm dea notting else is real. . . . My company wants to hire Miko fo' teach da touris' how to fish.

LISA: You didn't tell him that, did you?

ALIKA: Tell 'em? I wanted him fo' take it.

LISA: Alika, why! You know how much he hates haoles.

ALIKA: Why? What am I supposed to do?

LISA: I donno, maybe you have fishing rights. Where I grew up in Washington the Indians there had fishing rights.

ALIKA: Fishing rights? Dis is Hawai'i. Da Indians hea no get rights. Dis is one multimillion dolla deal. Nobody goin' give a damn dat two Hawaiian boys like keep fishing. Da only rights we get is fo' remain silent.

LISA: So what are you going to do?

ALIKA: What am I gonna do? Da's one good question. Up to now, Alika's just done what everybody tol' him fo' do. Da teacha tells Alika no cheat, so I no cheat—but I neva get one good job eidda. My cousins tell me fo' buy one boat, dat neva work. My boss tells me fo' work hard, spread da aloha, it's gonna pay off. Den dis is what I get—kick off my lan' so I can show da touris' where I used to live.

I donno. All I like do is keep my 'ohana togedda—four peopo'. Everybody tells me dis is paradise—how frickin' hard could it be fo' keep four peopo' togedda in paradise? Well, I can't let all dis shit jus' keep happening to me, ah? *(begins to exit)* I gotta go find Michael.

LISA: Alika? *(pause)* Nothing.

> *(LISA and STEVIE exit.)*

> *(MICHAEL in a cave, sitting, busily working on a shark-tooth dagger. ALIKA finds him.)*

ALIKA: Miko.

> *(MICHAEL ignores him.)*

Miko, I'm sorry fo' what I said. I neva mean fo' put you down li' dat. I jus' neva know what fo' do, da's all.

MICHAEL: Yeah, I know, 'Lika-Boy.

ALIKA: Miko, I only get you, Stevie an' Lisa lef'. I donno whea we goin' go but, I like you promise me you goin' stay wit' us.

MICHAEL: When Tūtū man was alive he wen' show me one secret. He brought me down to dis bay one day an' da bay was all black. Was da middo' of da day! Da wata outside was flat, but inside da bay da wata was all churning an' black. I got all scared, he wen' grab my hand an' take me in da wata. 'Lika-Boy, da bay was choke wit' 'ahi. Huge buggas, hundreds a' pounds, all ova! Thru ma legs, bumping me—dey was mating! Was unreal! So much fish like you neva seen befo'! Tūtū man brought me to dis cave. He tol' me sit down next to dis pōhaku—dis koʻa. I sat an' listen to him chant an' pray all day. Wen da sun started fo' go down, we wen' walk to da' ocean. Da bay was starting fo' calm down, I watched da 'ahi start fo' leave. He wen' in da' wata' an' stretch out his arms. He wen' straighten his back an lif' out one 'ahi big as him, da' fish wen' kick jus' once, an' den he went come home to us. Tūtū man tol' me ouwa family been here fo' generations, we wen take care deese fish from da time of Laʻamaikahiki. He tol' me, I was da next keepa of dis' koʻa. He tol' me, "Nāu e mālama i kēia kai a me kēia 'āina, i ola kuʻu 'ohana. Take care dis place and my family goin' live." Tūtū was a smart man, but he neva unnastan' what was coming. I took care dis place. I fed da fish when dey wen' come in. Twice a year we had 'ahi fo' fill ouwa 'ōpūs an' ouwa freezas. But one time, one tour boat wen fin' da school. I wen swim outside an' try fo stop 'em. But dose haoles, dey wen call everybody. Next ting I know, da bay stay full wit' peopo'—all kin' peopo. Dey had speas, baseball bats, machetes, shotgun—everyting. Was one frickin' slaughta! Peopo wen crazy, hacking an' shooting jus' fo' da' fun of it. By da time was ova, mos' a' da' fish was wasted. Afta I watched dat slaughta, I was so shame. I came hea an' prayed to Ke Akua dat he forgive us. Now, only little bit fish come back, maybe five, ten, an' not all da time. Some tings so ingrained, you cannot get ridda' it. Goin' take long time fo' teach dose fish dat now it's dangerous hea—every yea some still goin' die. Goin' take long time make Hawaiians no listen dea kūpuna.

ALIKA: Every year some still going die.

MICHAEL: Every year somting's gotta die. *(pause)* 'Lika-Boy, fo' you, Stevie, Georgie, Tūtū man and Tūtū wahine, all my 'ohana—I neva goin' leave this place. *(continues to work on the dagger)*

> *(ALIKA leaves.)*

SCENE 9

> *(ALIKA tries to dress but all the voices descend on him and he cannot. They taunt and confuse him. It is only when he "hears" his cousin MICHAEL chanting and humming that he can continue on.)*

ALIKA: To our left is 'Iolani Palace. You can visit the palace on our Hawaiian History Tour. 'Iolani Palace is the only royal palace within the boundaries of the United States. In 1893, Queen Lili'uokalani . . . *(pauses)* You know folks, when I joined this company, I was just outta high school. And when I started work they gave me speeches to memorize about the places that we would be visiting. But folks, today I'm having a hard time giving the speech about the palace because it's not true. You see, they want me to tell you that our last reigning monarch, Queen Lili'uokalani, wanted to give up her throne, her palace, and her kingdom to the United States for protection. Mostly because they don't want you to feel bad. They

think you're going to feel bad because what really
happened is that basically some American businessmen
backed by U.S. armed forces overthrew the Queen. They
took over our government, took away our rights as
Hawaiians and took our land. Nobody on this bus had
anything to do with that. I know that. But folks,
something really wrong happened. I mean, first we have
a kingdom, it's ours, the land's ours, and then all of a
sudden we got nothing. So I'm asking you, do you think
something wrong happened? I mean 'cause now, most of
us Hawaiians we don't have a place to live. But when it
was our country, we did.

   (silence)

MR. CLEMENTS: Hey, Mister Alika . . .

MRS. CLEMENTS: Now Henry, mind your manners.

MR. CLEMENTS: Mabel, I believe I have a right to speak my mind.
   Now son, you may remember me and my wife from a
   few days ago.

ALIKA: Yes, sir.

MR. CLEMENTS: Well, she was so impressed with your hospitality
   that she called your boss and specifically asked to have
   the rest of our tours with you. Mr. Alika, my wife and I
   have been saving twenty years to come here. And you
   know why? 'Cause everyone told us how nice it was here
   and how nice the people were. Twenty goddamn years!
   You know why we waited so long? 'Cause where we live
   it's pretty hard to make a goddamn living. I worked for a
   lotta years in the mines and I'm probably going to die of
   black lung from all the shit I had to breathe. . . .

ALIKA: Well, I'm not saying that—

MR. CLEMENTS: No, now you listen, you had your speech, you let
   me finish mine. Now those mines, the land they're on

used to belong to my family. But some big fat-ass company came in with their fancy-dancy lawyers and the next thing we know, we ain't got a home. But we got jobs in the mines now. So I watch my daddy go off to work in them mines. And I watch day after day and pretty soon I realize the work he's doing to feed us is killing him. And everytime he stuck food on the goddamn table I would look at him and wanna cry 'cause he was feeding us with his goddamn life. We didn't have much more than what we had on our table, on account of being such a big family, but my old man, he bought me a sweater once, beauty of a sweater. And I'd go out with it on all the time, but as soon as I got outta the house I'd take it off 'cause it felt like I had about two years of his life on my back. And when I got outta school, there weren't nothing to do in that goddamn town 'cept work in the mines. So me and the missus here, we ain't gonna have a big family, we gonna go to Hawaia for three weeks. And we're gonna do it while I still got lungs to breathe with. Nobody on this bus had anything to do with all of that, I know that. But goddamn it, I'm not giving up twenty years of my life just to hear some young punk tell me the United States of America took his goddamn palace. You don't know shit, kid. We all got sob stories. So now, why don't you just give us that speech we paid for?

MRS. CLEMENTS: Henry, sit down. You've made your point.

MR. CLEMENTS: Goddamn it to hell, Mabel. We save all this time and we don't even get to hear the goddamn speech!

ALIKA: *(to audience)* Here's where we get off. Watch your step when you exit. *(ALIKA steps off the bus, takes off his aloha shirt, throws it away.)*

> *(After a beat MRS. CLEMENTS gets up and follows ALIKA. ALIKA goes to the edge of the*

*stage, picks up some rocks, and begins to skip
them across the water. MRS. CLEMENTS comes
down and crosses to him.)*

MRS. CLEMENTS: You folks sure have a purty ocean.

(ALIKA does not answer.)

MRS. CLEMENTS: This is the first time I've ever seen the ocean
close up and personal. Oh, the smell of it, makes you feel
alive, don't it?

(ALIKA does not answer.)

MRS. CLEMENTS: Am I bothering you, honey?

(No answer.)

Well good, then I know you're gonna listen to every
word I say, whether you like it or not. And I don't mean
that unkindly either. You see, I know something's aching
in you, and I don't wanna see you hurt nobody,
'specially yourself.

ALIKA: Why do you care?

MRS. CLEMENTS: Why do I care? I care because I'm a Christian—a
Baptist to be exact. You know, so far as most white
Southern Baptists are concerned, there's only two kinds
of people in this world: white people—and everybody
else. But I don't agree with that. Jesus said some mighty
powerful things about loving everyone. But I'm a God-
fearing Baptist born and raised. Do you understand what
I'm telling you, son?

ALIKA: No. You sound just like my mother. She's always telling
me stories I don't understand.

MRS. CLEMENTS: My boy says the same thing to me. You see, I'm
an American history teacher. Did I tell you that? Well,
anyway, I'm a teacher. And I've got a pretty good idea of
what happened here about a hundred years ago—same

thing as happened in many places—and it ain't right. And I find myself married to a man who, God bless his soul, he is a fine and upstanding man but for the life of him, can't see, don't wanna see, and isn't ever gonna see that you're fighting for the same things he's fought for.

ALIKA: So what, you want me to know you're a Christian from a church that hates niggers and you're married to a blind man?

MRS. CLEMENTS: *(picks up a stone and tosses it across the water)* Funny you should say that, my boy says the same thing. God taught your ancestors how to live on this Earth better than any people I've ever studied. I guess he had to 'cause you folks are so far away from everything else. Oh dear, God bless you and keep you, Mister Alika Kealoha. I believe your people do sit in the Bosom of Abraham.

ALIKA: Oh, so what, we got land in Heaven?

MRS. CLEMENTS: I know, that sounds silly. I'm sorry. All I mean is I'm sorry.

ALIKA: Is that it, all you gotta say is you're sorry!

MRS. CLEMENTS: No, that's not all, but if you don't understand your mother then you're not gonna understand me. We're all blind Alika, some of us just know this better. And this world is an ugly place sometimes. When it all boils down it's about loving and being loved—and I believe—about aloha and sharing aloha. *(exits)*

> *(ALIKA stands, contemplating. He starts to make his way back. His BOSS comes down from the audience where he has been sitting.)*

BOSS: Alika!

ALIKA: *(stops)* I quit. I hate this job. I hate the lies I havta tell. I hate pimping my culcha. You don't care about

Hawaiians. You don't care dat we been hea foa centries. We ain't youa firs' concern—da bottom dalla, da's all you care about.

BOSS: So you haven't heard about your cousin?

ALIKA: What about him?

BOSS: He cut up two of our security guards today.

> *(MICHAEL is startled by the imaginary guards and goes for the sharktooth dagger. He mimes being kicked before reaching it.)*

He tried to kill them with a dagger.

> *(MICHAEL mimes being punched, kicked, dragged up against a wall and handcuffed.)*

Lucky for him they were able to subdue him. If he had killed someone. . . .

> *(MICHAEL mimes being unhandcuffed and put in a cell.)*

He'd never see the light of day again. So you're quitting, huh? And I don't care about Hawaiians? You stupid kanaka. I just spent three hours in there trying to convince the board that you had nothing to do with this.

ALIKA: That's just 'cause I can make money for you.

BOSS: Fuck you! I stuck my neck out for you. Gave them my personal apology. They wanted you outta your house in forty-eight hours. You still don't get it, do you. It's not your land and these aren't your islands anymore. The game's survival. I've got a family to feed and so do you. And no matter what we do, they're gonna keep building. So you wanna quit? Don't. *(exits)*

<u>SCENE 10</u>

*(ALIKA walks into MICHAEL's area. MICHAEL
unfreezes and mimes coming out of his cell.
The two cousins face each other.)*

ALIKA: You arright in hea? You know I quit my job? I quit 'cause I
was going come back fishing wit you. I figured we could
find some new grounds an' between me an' you we
could take care Stevie. Now what! Now I'm on my own.
You're all da frickin family I got left! An' when we're all
dead, den what? *(looks around prison)* You call this living?
(pause. Turns to leave.)

(Hears voices.)

MICHAEL: Alika, come visit me, ah. Lonely in hea.

BOSS: *(vo)* So you're quitting, huh? You stupid kanaka.

MRS. YAMAMOTO: *(vo)* Alika, we're waiting.

ALIKA: Leave me alone!

(LISA and STEVIE enter.)

STEVIE: Uncle!

ALIKA: Sorry Stevie, Uncle's got plenty fo' do. Jus' go finish youa
homework.

MOM: *(vo)* Not at the bottom of a bottle!

ALIKA: Stop it!

LISA: We didn't say anything! Alika, did you hear what
happened?

ALIKA: *(nods)* I quit my job.

LISA: What?

ALIKA: You heard me, I quit. *(pours himself a glass and gulps it down)*

> *(From now until* ALIKA *takes* STEVIE *to shrine, the voices come down on him, building to a nerve-wracking crescendo.)*

LISA: Damn it, you! Your niece needs you. You and Michael are the closest thing to a father she's ever had. Now Michael's in jail and you're out of a job and a place to live! How're you gonna take care of her now, huh? What kind of role models has she got? There's a right way and a wrong way to do things.

ALIKA: Lisa, you're a haole, you don't unnerstan.

LISA: Oh, here it comes.

ALIKA: That's right. I got a history, an' I ain't gonna work for a company dat's gonna take away everything I love.

LISA: And since I'm haole I can't understand that.

ALIKA: You don't have a history, you ran away from yours. Besides, your family hasn't been on their land for generations.

LISA: No. And I don't know who anybody past my grandparents were. And even though I never met your kūpuna, I loved them through the stories George told me. But I'm haole—and so is my daughter. . . . Alika, you think your pain is special, it's not. You think your history's the ugliest—it's not! It's your love, it's your aloha that's special! That's why the world keeps coming in on you!

ALIKA: *(pours another glass)* Well, I ain't got anymore fucking aloha, okay!

MOM: *(vo)* You're not gonna find the answers there.

ALIKA: Leave me alone!

LISA: Okay!

ALIKA: I didn't mean you. I'm sorry, I'm just . . . I'm sorry.

MRS. YAMAMOTO: *(vo)* Alika, please lead us in the Pledge of Allegiance!

(*ALIKA turns, trying to place the voice.*)

LISA: Alika, I really need, um . . .

ALIKA: I gotta get all our stuff together.

LISA: I know, but . . . *(starts to break down)* Alika, I'm not sure that . . . Please! My daughter, she loves her uncles so much! Alika, I don't know. . . .

ALIKA: Stop crying, okay! We got a lot of work to do.

MOM: *(vo)* That's it, push her.

ALIKA: Shut up already!

LISA: I'm sorry, I'm sorry! I didn't mean to . . . why are you always so mean to me! What do you want? You want me to just give you my daughter? Is that what you want?

ALIKA: Lisa, I'm sorry, okay. I'm just having a hard time keeping everything together.

LISA: You're having a hard time? What about me? Don't you think I'm having a hard time, too. Don't you think I love Michael too!

BOSS: *(vo)* You still don't get it do you? It's not your land and these aren't your islands anymore.

ALIKA: *(to BOSS)* Fuck you!

LISA: Alika!

STEVIE: Uncle, whea we goin stay now?

ALIKA: I'll handle it. Don't worry, just go to sleep.

LISA: Alika, stop it, you're scaring me!

MICHAEL: *(vo)* 'Lika-Boy, you da one dat keeps us togedda.

BOSS: *(vo)* I stuck my neck out for you! Gave them my personal apology!

LISA: Alika, please, sit down!

SECURITY GUARD: *(vo)* I'm really sorry but the management would like you all to leave.

ALIKA: Leave me alone.

MOM: *(vo)* Kāmau. Pono au e kāmau. Say it!

ALIKA: I'm tired Mama, I just wanna go sleep!

LISA: *(runs over to ALIKA)* Alika! What's wrong with you? Sit down.

ALIKA: *(to LISA)* Sit down? Sit down? What fo'? Da management would like us all to leave.

MRS. CLEMENTS: *(vo)* You all seem to get along just fine . . .

GEORGE: *(vo)* Nah, cuz, no worry, I strong!

MRS. YAMAMOTO: *(vo)* Your cousins can't get you a job or put food on your plate.

ALIKA: They did!

LISA: Alika, Alika, listen to me. It's gonna be alright. We can make it. Okay. You've just been drinking too much.

STEVIE: I'm hungry. Can we eat now?

MICHAEL: *(vo)* You like beef!

GEORGE: *(vo)* No, I like chicken!

ALIKA: Stevie, I donno, I'm kinda, I gotta . . .

LISA: Alika, you're hallucinating, please, sit down!

BOSS: *(vo)* The game's survival.

GEORGE: *(vo)* Da tree muskateas of da ocean!

MICHAEL: *(vo)* Us guys, we stupid.

ALIKA: Mama, I'm tired.

MOM: *(vo)* I know son. But you cannot give up.

LISA: Alika, please, sit down, you're gonna hurt yourself!

ALIKA: I'm having a hard time.

LISA: I know, just sit.

MOM: *(vo)* Pono au e kāmau! Say it! You must carry on, Alika Kaleihaʻaheoʻonākūpuna!

MRS CLEMENTS: *(vo)* When it all boils down, it's about aloha.

MOM: *(vo)* Your aloha for life, don't lose it. It's all we got!

LISA: Alika, please! Please! Please! We need you! *(clings to him, hitting him.)* Stop killing yourself! Don't leave my daughter with nothing! Don't let her suffer like you. Please.

MICHAEL: *(vo)* Come visit me, ah, ʻLika-Boy. Lonely in hea.

GEORGE: *(vo)* Lonely out hea.

ALIKA: *(grabbing STEVIE's arms, stopping her, holding her)* I'm tired of losing everybody I love.

MOM: *(vo)* It's a big mess, my boy. But you've gotta carry it 'cause your ʻohana is depending on you. Kāmau. Carry on. Say it.

STEVIE: Uncle, you hurt so much because everybody you love leaves you. You want me to hurt like that too?

ALIKA: No. I love you Stevie. I don't want you to hurt like me. Kāmau.

LISA: What? What did you say?

ALIKA: Kāmau. It means to carry on.

STEVIE: Uncle, where we going?

ALIKA: Kulikuli.

> *(ALIKA and STEVIE enter the cave.)*

Sit down. This is our koʻa, our fishing shrine. Whatever happens we must take care of it.

STEVIE: Yes, Uncle.

ALIKA: Time for you to learn how to patch net . . .

MOM: *(vo)* Maopopo ʻia ʻoe i kēia manawa o kou tūtū moʻolelo? Now do you understand what Tūtū was trying to say?

ALIKA: 'Cause there's always gonna be holes in youa net. *(picks up his uniform and puts it back on.)*

> *(MICHAEL paces his cell.)*

ALIKA: Aloooohaaa!

> *(waits for a response from the audience, is not satisfied, invites the audience to respond.)*

Alooohaa!

> *(audience responds)*

Mahalo, and welcome to your Aloha Tours' "Guide to Oʻahu." My name's Alika and I'll be your host for today. At the helm is Big Al—best darn bus driver this side of Hollywood. This is our Historical Sights Tour and the first place we'll be going to is the Arizona Memorial. From there we'll head on over to ʻIolani Palace Grounds for lunch and end up at Punchbowl Cemetery, National Memorial of the Pacific. We at Aloha Tours are here to serve you, so if you have any questions at all, just ask!

> *(lights out)*

GLOSSARY

āholehole – young stage of the āhole fish

'ae – yes

'ahi – tuna

'āina – land

Errytings rad. – Everything is perfect. (Pidgin)

haole(s) – foreigner, also used disparagingly to mean "white"

hāpai – pregnant

he'e – octopus

He mau kaona kēia – These things have hidden meanings

hoe – a paddle or to paddle

howsit – "How is it going?" (Pidgin)

Kaleiha'aheo'onākūpuna – Proud lei of the ancestors

kanaka – Hawaiian man

Ke Akua – God

ko'a – stone fishing shrine

kulikuli – shut up, be quiet

kupuna – a grandparent and generation of same

lōlō – stupid

mahalo – thank you

mākaukau – ready?

mālie – calm, as in ocean

"Me ke aloha, ku'u home o Kahalu'u" – "With warm aloha for my home in Kahalu'u"

moi – threadfish

moke – Hawaiian redneck

mo'o – lizard or supernatural serpent/dragon

"Nāu e mālama i kēia kai a me kēia 'āina, i ola ku'u 'ohana." – "Yours is the responsibility to care for this ocean and this land, (and if you do) your family will thrive."

nuha – angry, sullen

"O ko'u na'au, ko'u 'ohana a me ka 'ōlelo Hawai'i. 'Ae, 'ōlelo au i ka 'ōlelo makuahine. A 'o 'oe?" – "My guts, my family and the Hawaiian language. Yes, I speak the mother tongue. What about you?"

'ohana – the family in any context

'ōkole – buttocks (Hawaiian slang)

'o'opu – freshwater goby

'ōpū – stomach

pakalōlō – marijuana, *Cannabis sativa*

pau – finished

pīlau – stink

pōhaku – stones, boulders

"Pono 'oe e ho'okāmau." – "You have to carry the burden and continue on."

pūne'e – backless movable couch

"Tsā, he pelapela wale nō." – "All you have is a dirty mouth."

pukapuka – many holes

Tūtū man – grandfather (Pidgin)

ua pau – it is finished

uhu – parrotfish

wahine – woman

"You like beef?" – "Do you want to fight?" (Pidgin)

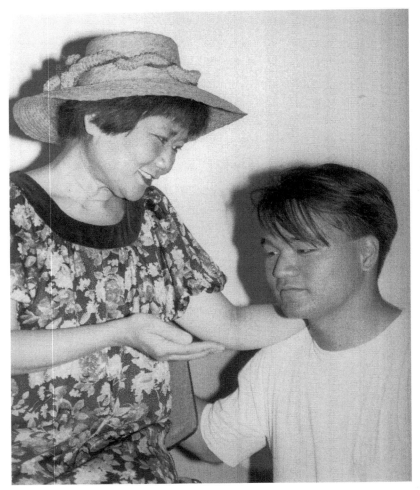

Nyla Fujii, Charles Timtim.

Alani Apio is a woodcarver, actor, dramatist/writer, visual artist and currently a director in community and public relations for a local public relations firm. His play *Kāmau* toured with Kumu Kahua Theatre in 1993–1994 and *Kāmau A'e*, the second part of the *Kāmau* trilogy, was produced by Kumu Kahua in 1997. His poetry has been featured in *Hawai'i Review* and his short story work in *The Best of Honolulu Fiction* (stories from the *HONOLULU Magazine* fiction contest [Bamboo Ridge Press 1999]). *Kāmau* appeared in excerpted form in *'Ōiwi: A Native Hawaiian Journal*, Vol. 1. His articles on Hawaiian sovereignty, multiculturalism, and race and ethnic relations have appeared in several national publications as well as in *The Honolulu Advertiser*.

Sponsored by **ALEXANDER & BALDWIN FOUNDATION**

KUMU KAHUA THEATRE PRESENTS

AS PART OF ITS THIRTIETH ANNIVERSARY SEASON
THE WORLD PREMIERE OF

KUPUA

Two Traditional Hawaiian Stories of Shape-Shifters

Illustration by Mike Harada

by Tammy Haili'ōpua Baker
Directed by Harry Wong, III

Sensual and sexy folk-tales, with gnashing of hula and chant, charting the phenomenon of Hawaiian 'shape-shifters' – spirits of anarchic nature which inhabit the forms of animals by day and human erotic partners by night, and mesmerize and 'hollow-out' the objects of their attentions. A fascinating window onto some of the lesser-known aspects of Hawaiian culture.

Please note: This play contains adult situations.

8:00 pm: March 15, 16, 22, 23, 24, 29, 30, 31; April 5, 6, 7, 12, 13, 14, 2001
2:00 pm: March 18, 25; April 1, 8, 15, 2001

ADMISSION:
Fridays, Saturdays and Sundays: $15 General, $12 Seniors and
Groups of 10 or more, $10 Students
Thursdays: $12 General, $10 Seniors & Unemployed, $5 Students

KUMU KAHUA
T H E A T R E
46 Merchant Street
(Corner of Merchant and Bethel)

BOX OFFICE: 536-4441
Box Office and Phone Line open
Monday through Friday 11:00AM – 3:00PM

Public parking for performances is available in the
Harbor Court Building, across the street from the theatre.

Kumu Kahua productions are supported
by the State Foundation on Culture and
the Arts celebrating more than thirty years
of culture and the arts in Hawai'i;
the Mayor's Office of Culture and Arts,
Jeremy Harris, Mayor;
The Hawaii Community Foundation and
Foundations, Businesses and Patrons.

Kupua:
Shape Shifting
J. Wat

Kupua, printed here, is a Pidgin (Hawaiian Creole English) play based on two traditional stories, *Ka 'Enuhe* and *Ka Puhi a me Ka Loli.* Baker credits *"Ka'ao Hawai'i,* traditional stories collected and told by Mary Kawena Pukui, *Na Ka'ao Kahiko* and other *mānaleo* (native speakers) who have shared these *mo'olelo* (stories or traditions) generation after generation."

Baker says that she chooses traditional material "because it's a resource that we can learn from and there's so much out there, that in my lifetime, I'll only scratch the surface." She adds that, "[w]e can learn about the value system in traditional Hawai'i, which is different today, those lessons are valuable as well."

Harry Wong, who directed the premiere production for Kumu Kahua says that one of the attractions for presenting the plays was "the light-hearted way in which Tammy treats the stories so it's like the culture isn't dead. It's still developing; we can still make use of it to express something different or another cultural value that is important. The art form, the stories, are still living and so we use them and we change them."

"Every culture's myths," Wong says, "are always reinterpreted by the upcoming generation to make it pertinent for today."

Wong, drawing from Bruno Bettelheim's *Uses of Enchantment* adds that, "[t]he hope is that these are kind of adult myths even though they might seem 'kiddie' at first. There's a kind of darkness. It's only recently that myths have become sanitized. It's not that kids have less passion or fear; they even have more but they can't deal with it. The myth, the story, provides a way for them to express it and work their way through it and I think Tammy is dealing with these myths and trying to do the same thing."

Although well known for writing and directing plays in the Hawaiian language with her own company, Kā Hālau Hanakeaka, Baker says that she writes plays in three languages: Hawaiian, English, and Pidgin. As for the differences in the writing process, she says that "[o]n the Hawaiian side, there's a little more research that goes into it, and there's a little more double checking language and stuff like that. The Pidgin is just reading it and making sure it's what I would consider authentic, growing up that being my first language. And then the English, I think, is always bouncing it off somebody else. 'How dis one sound?'"

When asked to comment on how being Hawaiian affects her writing, Baker responds that, "[t]he idea of *kuleana* goes into play, the obvious part, the stories that are chosen, the material. But then having this kind of responsibility to uphold tradition, look to the past to guide the future." She adds that, "we can capture that in traditional cultural practice and also the perpetuation of the language." Finally, she notes that as a Hawaiian, "it's your responsibility to make sure this stuff is passed down to the next generation."

Wong notes that while writing plays so close to the culture can sometimes be exclusionary, "Tammy, being a person of the theatre, wants to be as inclusive as much as possible." Baker, therefore draws, not only from her Hawaiian heritage, but also from her experiences as an actor and director, to make the play work for a wide audience. She comments: "I always feel like I'm wearing a number of hats. When I write something, I don't think it's just words on a page. It's something that I've looked at from many different angles: as a director, will it work? And then as an actor, can this be said in such a way or can I do something with my body instead? So I think that's continuously happening.

Is this a viable piece of material? Is there dramatic action? Can we put this on the stage?"

And looking to traditional sources for inspiration, she adds, "I think every *mo'olelo*, every story I read, I think like that."

Wong speculates that Baker's theatre is made possible by a new kind of actor. "People like Nara [Springer] and Lani-Girl [Waiau], maybe even 'Āina [Rapoza, cast members of the premiere production of *Kupua*], it's only now that [the theatre has] people who can chant and dance hula and who can act." Wong notes that *Kupua* is "partially written for people who can do all that." On the other hand, Wong speculates that Baker's work is "beginning to not only create the plays but beginning to create the people who can do all this." "And," he adds, "they're not necessarily all Hawaiian."

While Baker's play is comprehensively scripted, much of what appears on stage is brought there by the director and the actors. Baker also draws from her multifaceted theatre experience and her cultural background to speak about her ideas concerning the value of process in producing a play. "That's always the exciting part, the process of getting there. After the script is written, there's just this awesome journey that you take part in. It's always a work in process. I'm never stuck with what's on the page, it's like a guide, not etched in stone. The choice to do that is to make the story accessible. When you come from an oral tradition, it needs to be alive for everybody."

'Āina Rapoza, Squire Coldwell, Ed Duncan.

KUPUA

BY

TAMMY HAILI'ŌPUA BAKER

Kupua was first produced by Kumu Kahua Theatre in Honolulu
on March 15, 2001. The production was directed by Harry
Wong III with the following cast:

Ka 'Enuhe (The Caterpillar)

WAIPUNA . . . . .Nara Mālia Mio Springer
KUMUHEA . . . . .Ed Kalā Duncan
KAWAI . . . . .Kameha'ililani Waiau
'ENUHE . . . . .Squire F. Coldwell
. . . . .Ely Wyatt Na Ka Ulu 'Āina Rapoza

Ka Puhi a me Ka Loli (The Eel and the Sea Cucumber)

KAPUHI . . . . .Ely Wyatt Na Ka Ulu 'Āina Rapoza
'ANAPAU . . . . .Nara Mālia Mio Springer
KALOLI . . . . .Squire F. Coldwell
KILIPUE . . . . .Kameha'ililani Waiau
KA'UPENA . . . . .Ed Kalā Duncan
THE MUSICIAN . . . . .Monica Cho

Set Design: Storm Stafford
Light Design: Cora Yamagata
Costume Design: BullDog
Prop Design: John H. Y. Wat
Assistant Director/Stage Manager: Meredith Desha

90   HE LEO HOU — A NEW VOICE

KA ʻENUHE

CHARACTERS (in order of appearance)

KUMUHEA—a *kupua*, son of Kū, he's a man during the day and a
 large *ʻenuhe* (caterpillar) during the night

WAIPUNA—**KUMUHEA**'s wife

KAWAI—father of **WAIPUNA**

a *kahu* (care giver or honored attendant) of **KAWAI**

two actors who make up the *ʻenuhe* body during the
 transformation scenes

TIME: Traditional Hawaiʻi

PLACE: Ka Moku o Keawe

SETTING: The stage is rather bare, divided into three locations.

> SL is the home of KUMUHEA and WAIPUNA. A mat signifies the interior and sleeping area. A tree stump (for securing a rope) near the home is necessary for the final scene.

> SR is KAWAI's home.

> Between these two areas are large sweet potato patches.

> Note: Set is minimal. Focus on the lighting to distinguish one environment from another, create special effects, and show the passing of time.

SOURCE FOR MATERIAL: *Kaʻao Hawaiʻi*, traditional stories collected and told by Mary Kawena Pukui, *Nā Kaʻao Kahiko* and other *mānaleo* (native speakers) who have shared this *moʻolelo* (story or tradtion) generation after generation.

> This is a Hawaiian Creole English (HCE) play.

SCENE 1

(The dim lights reveal a woman, WAIPUNA, sleeping on her side. She rolls over, reaching for her husband who isn't there. She reaches her arm as far as she can to feel for him. She turns to her side and snuggles up to her kapa [blanket]. She returns to sleep. Her body is still. Her husband, KUMUHEA, sneaks back into the house and under the covers. KUMUHEA rolls over to her to make his presence known. WAIPUNA turns over to him and snuggles up to him. They return to sleep and the lights fade out.)

SCENE 2

(Lights up. It is the next morning. WAIPUNA is with KUMUHEA. He is very large compared to her. They sit and talk for a bit. She is very affectionate to him. He barely moves. KUMUHEA's personality is similar to the modern-day moke.)

WAIPUNA: Eh Kumuhea, last night I had one dream.

KUMUHEA: *(surprised)* One dream?

WAIPUNA: 'Ae. I had dream that I was sleeping. . . .

KUMUHEA: *(listening closely)* And?

WAIPUNA: Well I was sleeping and you had . . .

KUMUHEA: *(looking more at WAIPUNA)* I had . . .

WAIPUNA: Well, *(pause)* you no was there.

KUMUHEA: Aiya, what kine dream is that?

WAIPUNA: I don't know? *(She watches his reactions very carefully.)* That's why I wanted for tell you about 'um.

KUMUHEA: Funny kine that dream. *(beat)* But you know what, no worry. You no worry about that kine stuff because I right here with you.

> *(Taps WAIPUNA on her shoulder like a man would smack one of his buddies on the shoulder area.)*

I going take good care of you, you no more nothing for worry about.

WAIPUNA: I hope so!

> *(WAIPUNA smiles and cuddles up to KUMUHEA. She nudges him and hints for him to put his arms around her. He doesn't catch on. WAIPUNA grabs his arm and places it around her. KUMUHEA pulls her in tightly, but it's very uncomfortable for her. She tries to make the best of the moment. Eventually WAIPUNA pulls away because of his tight crunch-like embrace. KUMUHEA smiles at her as if he's "Mr. Romance." She's totally disappointed but nevertheless she fakes a smile. KUMUHEA stretches and yawns. He attempts to take a nap while WAIPUNA looks around their living area for something to eat.)*

WAIPUNA: Kumuhea, I small kine hungry.

KUMUHEA: Hungry.

WAIPUNA: 'Ae. *(beat)* You not hungry?

KUMUHEA: Me? Hungry? *(beat)* No.

WAIPUNA: Well, I stay real hungry.

KUMUHEA: And what?

WAIPUNA: Well, I was thinking . . . maybe you was going get me some food for eat?

KUMUHEA: Me?

WAIPUNA: 'Ae, you my husband. You poss to [supposed to] take care of me, right?

KUMUHEA: *(shaking his head)* Yeah, and what? No more one roof over your head?

WAIPUNA: Get but *(beat)* I still hungry.

KUMUHEA: Ho I tired, I going sleep.

> *(KUMUHEA lies down right where he's sitting and tries to go to sleep. WAIPUNA is upset and leans over him. She stares him down.)*

KUMUHEA: What you doing?

> *(WAIPUNA stares at KUMUHEA.)*

KUMUHEA: Come on babe, I tired . . . maybe later.

WAIPUNA: What? You think that's what I like? Hemo skin! Brah I hungry, I no like hump right now! I like eat!

KUMUHEA: Eat? Again?

WAIPUNA: What you mean *again*? I never eat for how many days already!

KUMUHEA: No, I mean you complaining for eat *again*!

> *(WAIPUNA is totally upset. KUMUHEA lies back down to sleep.)*

WAIPUNA: *(trying to calm down)* Alright. Whatever—

KUMUHEA: *(sitting up)* You know what, you so hungry, why you no go and get something for eat? *(acts all macho)* Yeah you can get your own food! *(returns to sleep)*

WAIPUNA: I no can believe you. *(under her breath)* You so fricken lazy. *(beat)* Sit on your ass all fricken day!

> *(She shakes her head and watches KUMUHEA sleep.)*

I should of never—no never mind, I going see my dad. Garrans get food over there.

> *(Lights fade out on KUMUHEA sleeping and follows WAIPUNA who crosses over to her father's place. Lights up on KAWAI. He is meditating. WAIPUNA approaches. KAWAI sees her, he stands and calls her in to his home area.)*

KAWAI: Hūi e Waipuna, e komo mai, he mai he mai.

> *(WAIPUNA walks up to KAWAI. They honi [a traditional Hawaiian greeting somewhere between a kiss and an exchange of breath] and hug.)*

KAWAI: How's my daughter? You can tell me after, you go eat first. Come, come eat. We get some ʻono kine sweet potato today.

> *(A kahu brings in a tray filled with traditional foods for WAIPUNA. She immediately starts eating, shoveling piece after piece into her mouth.)*

So nice to see you Waipuna.

> *(She nods in agreement.)*

Eh get plenty food honey. You eat up!

(She continues to stuff her face, clearing nearly everything off of the platter.)

How about something for drink?

(KAWAI signals to the kahu. *The* kahu *brings over a* huewai *[gourd for carrying water] and a wooden cup. The* kahu *pours a cup of water for WAIPUNA and hands it to KAWAI.)*

(to kahu*)* Mahalo.

(WAIPUNA has finished the food and is wiping her mouth as KAWAI hands her the cup. She drinks.)

You seem pretty hungry. You like little more food?

(KAWAI signals to his kahu. *WAIPUNA shakes her head "no" as she finishes the water.)*

You sure?

WAIPUNA: 'Ae, mahalo this was real 'ono!

KAWAI: So how you been? How you and Kumuhea doing?

WAIPUNA: Maika'i.

KAWAI: You sure? You say that like you not too sure.

WAIPUNA: Nah we good Daddy. But actually I no can stay too long. I get some stuff for do.

KAWAI: Oh yeah? What you get for do?

WAIPUNA: I just wanted for say hello, yeah.

KAWAI: So what you get for do?

WAIPUNA: Well, 'um, I was thinking about going da kine. . . .

KAWAI: What kine?

WAIPUNA: Ah, what you call that? Ah—

KAWAI: I don't know?

WAIPUNA: I no can remember.

KAWAI: For real? *(beat)* You sure you never come here for talk to me about something?

> *(WAIPUNA messes with her hair and rubs her neck.)*

Something wrong? You guys having pilikia?

> *(WAIPUNA looks down, she is obviously troubled. KAWAI approaches her, he puts his arm around her.)*

Baby Girl, if there's something wrong, talk to me. Maybe I can kōkua?

> *(WAIPUNA hesitates.)*

Baby, remember Daddy is here for you.

WAIPUNA: I know. *(long pause)* Maybe I see you tomorrow Dad.

KAWAI: *(nodding)* Okay. *(reaches over and embraces his daughter)* Here baby, why you no take home little bit food for you and Kumuhea.

> *(The kahu brings a pūʻolo [a wrapped bundle of food] and presents it to KAWAI, who hands it to WAIPUNA.)*

Here, it's just a little something, for snack or whatever.

> *(They honi. WAIPUNA exits. Lights out on KAWAI watching her leave.)*

SCENE 3

(Lights up on KUMUHEA who is lounging around the house. He seems tired and frustrated. The sun begins to set. WAIPUNA returns home.)

WAIPUNA: *(under her breath)* Sleeping again.

(WAIPUNA sits down and opens the pūʻolo. KUMUHEA tosses and stretches. He seems to be awake. WAIPUNA takes some of the food out and offers it to KUMUHEA. He is not interested.)

WAIPUNA: You sure?

KUMUHEA: Yeah, yeah, yeah I no like, I no like.

(long pause. WAIPUNA munches on the sweet potato.)

WAIPUNA: So what you did today?

KUMUHEA: Me?

WAIPUNA: No, the man in the loʻi.

KUMUHEA: Gee! No catch a rash.

WAIPUNA: So what you did?

KUMUHEA: Cruz.

WAIPUNA: So you had sleep all day?

KUMUHEA: *(takes a deep breath)* No, why?

WAIPUNA: *(irritated)* Just checking.

KUMUHEA: Eh, no act like that!

(The following sequence is used to show the passing of time from sunset into the evening. The actors move around for ten to fifteen seconds and then hold a position for five

seconds. This happens three to five times and with each frozen tableau the lights dim to signify the passing of time. The two actors should progress from one evening ritual to another. (The modern equivalent would be; having dinner, watching some television, taking a shower, brushing teeth.) *The final frozen tableau consists of both actors on a sleeping mat going to sleep. Instrumental music should be layered under the action. At the end of the sequence, the couple is in "bed" and exchange bedtime wishes.)*

KUMUHEA: Good night my dear.

> *(KUMUHEA seems to have a burst of energy)*

WAIPUNA: Good night Kumuhea.

KUMUHEA: Sweet dreams. *(remembering her dream)* Ah no maybe you no like dream, yeah? Have a good sleep. I see you in the morning.

> *(WAIPUNA rolls her eyes. KUMUHEA hugs her, gripping her arms as in the opening scene. WAIPUNA is agitated. KUMUHEA releases her. He lies on his back for a second. KUMUHEA scratches his head and rubs his belly contemplating his next move. Then suddenly KUMUHEA lifts himself above her and starts kissing her. WAIPUNA pulls away. He's frisky and persistent, trying to make a move on her. He stumbles with each attempt to initiate sex. WAIPUNA finds humor in his clumsiness and is slightly aroused by his determination. They tumble around and simulate making love. After their encounter, WAIPUNA dozes off. KUMUHEA is totally wired. He waits, watching to see she is fast asleep. KUMUHEA grabs her arm and it is*

limp. She is in a deep sleep. KUMUHEA lifts her arm again to double check. The arm falls completely limp. KUMUHEA slowly and smoothly sneaks out of bed. He adjusts his kapa. KUMUHEA looks at her and then leaves. WAIPUNA continues to sleep. The lights are dim.

Two actors who form the ʻenuhe body gradually appear on the side of KUMUHEA. Traditional Hawaiian musical instruments are heard. KUMUHEA transforms into a ʻenuhe [caterpillar]. His body length will triple as the ʻenuhe body attaches to him. The transformation is a mock hula. The music sets a rhythm for KUMUHEA's movement. His moves are similar to a kāholo [hula vamp]. KUMUHEA is not very agile on his feet; he is a novice hula dancer. His movements are somewhat comical. The ʻenuhe body also moves in a hula style as they attach their arms to KUMUHEA extending and enlarging KUMUHEA's silhouette to create the ʻenuhe. KUMUHEA's posture and mannerisms are that of a caterpillar. The actors are now completely joined, moving as one large ʻenuhe. The large body moves along the stage as a caterpillar arching its body up and down in order to travel. This is reminiscent of the "worm" dance move from the early 80s dance style "Popping" or "Break Dancing." The rhythm of the music adjusts to this kind of movement, using the traditional hula instruments in a more modern beat.

Lights up on the sweet potato patches. KUMUHEA begins to eat all of the sweet potato leaves in sight. [Note: The sweet potato leaves

*should not be realistic.] During KUMUHEA's
feasting, the 'enuhe body actors occasionally
extend their arms or legs to break up the leaves
in the patches and create a crunching sound.
As KUMUHEA devours the leaves, WAIPUNA
turns over and feels for KUMUHEA. WAIPUNA
awakes to see that he is gone. He is nowhere to
be found in their home.)*

WAIPUNA: Kumuhea? *(long pause)* Kumuhea? *(pause)* Kumuhea, where you stay? *(shakes her head)* Where did that lazy ass go? Frick! *(She returns to sleep.)*

*(KUMUHEA continues to eat through the sweet
potato patches. Lights out.)*

SCENE 4

*(Lights up, it is very early in the morning.
WAIPUNA is still asleep. KUMUHEA returns
home. He sneaks in very slowly. Carefully
KUMUHEA lifts the kapa and slips into bed.
WAIPUNA turns away from him. KUMUHEA
moves closer and attempts to snuggle. She pulls
away. KUMUHEA passes out with his arm across
her body. WAIPUNA wakes up and moves his
arm off. KUMUHEA snores. WAIPUNA gets out of
bed and looks for breakfast. There's a little
piece of kalo [taro] left. She eats it and is on
the verge of crying. WAIPUNA walks over to
KUMUHEA and contemplates inflicting some
sort of pain on him but can not figure out what
to do. Frustrated, she leaves for her father's
home.*

*Lights cross-fade to KAWAI. He is meditating
again. WAIPUNA approaches. KAWAI notices
her and immediately calls her in.)*

KAWAI: E komo mai e ku'u keiki ē, e Waipuna, ku'u kaikamahine.

> *(WAIPUNA runs up to KAWAI and embraces
> him. He holds her and consoles her.)*

Tell me what's wrong sweetie.

WAIPUNA: It's Kumuhea Daddy. I no know what for do.

KAWAI: What's wrong?

WAIPUNA: Three nights already, he been dig after we go sleep. I
when even ask him about 'um, I told him I had one
dream that he no was there when I was sleeping, and
him, he when just pretend like he never know nothing.
He said my dream was *funny kine*! But I think he been
sneaking out for be with somebody else, cause he come
home so tired, he sleep all day, no do nothing, he no
even eat, he no even feed me! I thought that's what
husbands supposed to do, take care of their wife. . . .
Right? *(saddened)* I just no know what for do.

KAWAI: It's okay.

WAIPUNA: I don't know? I don't know how come he acting like
this for?

KAWAI: No worry sweetie. I gonna help you. Maybe you eat
something now.

> *(The kahu enters with a tray of food and sets it
> before WAIPUNA.)*

WAIPUNA: Mahalo.

KAWAI: You eat and relax.

WAIPUNA: Mahalo Dad. *(eats heartily)*

(KAWAI stands and moves to the kahu. *KAWAI whispers his plan to the* kahu. *The* kahu *nods and exits. KAWAI returns to WAIPUNA.)*

KAWAI: Listen honey, Daddy has a idea so we can find out where Kumuhea been going at night.

WAIPUNA: *(stops eating and listens)* Okay.

KAWAI: Tonight when you two go sleep,

(WAIPUNA nods. The following dialogue fades out with the lights.)

you going have to stay awake until Kumuhea falls asleep, then you going need for—

(There is a cross-fade to KUMUHEA who is sleeping as usual. WAIPUNA enters and notices that he is asleep.)

WAIPUNA: Cutting kiawes again. All he do is sleep. *(pause)* Must have been one hard night last night! *(leaves the home and approaches the tree stump. She removes a rope from her* pā'ū *[traditional Hawaiian skirt], given to her from KAWAI. While fastening the rope to the tree, WAIPUNA talks to herself, she rattles off the following lines quickly.)* This going be Kumuhea's last night out, that's for sure! Damn lazy ass, he just wait till I find out where he been going! Lazy ass, sleep all day, good for nothing! *(pulling the rope tight)* No can work. No can get me food. Only sleep. Sleep, sleep, sleep all day long. And then, night time come, *pau!* He gone, sneaking his fat lazy ass out of bed! He think I don't know. That is it! *(The rope is fastened.)* I had it already! *(hides the remaining rope on the other side of the tree)* He wait, I going fix his ass good!

(KUMUHEA awakes from his daily sleep. WAIPUNA re-enters the home.)

KUMUHEA: Eh love, where you been?

WAIPUNA: I went walking.

KUMUHEA: Walking.

WAIPUNA: Yeah, walking.

KUMUHEA: Good, good, good. *(stands, stretches, and rubs his belly)*

WAIPUNA: *(approaching KUMUHEA)* Eh Kumuhea, you ever heard about sleepwalking?

KUMUHEA: Ah no!

WAIPUNA: I heard sometimes people, when they sleeping, they get up and just walk any kine places.

KUMUHEA: For real?

WAIPUNA: Yeah, for real!

KUMUHEA: You know funny kine but, I stay real tired. I think I going back sleep.

WAIPUNA: Eh Kumuhea, the sun still stay up. Look, she going down slow, why we no enjoy the sunset together, heh?

KUMUHEA: Uh—

WAIPUNA: Come on Kumuhea.

KUMUHEA: Uh . . . okay.

(WAIPUNA moves in close to KUMUHEA)

WAIPUNA: See, nice yeah the sky?

KUMUHEA: Uh yeah, I guess so. *(pause)* You sure you no like take one nap?

WAIPUNA: *(looking at him)* Kumuhea!

KUMUHEA: Gee, no need give me the eye!

(The same sequence from SCENE 3 is used here to show the passing of time and the setting of the sun. However this time each tableau has

> WAIPUNA *and* KUMUHEA *interacting with one another. Again the final tableau is of them in bed going to sleep.)*

WAIPUNA: Good night sweetheart.

KUMUHEA: *(exhausted)* Yeah, good night.

WAIPUNA: See you in the morning.

KUMUHEA: *(nearly asleep)* Yeah, morning.

> *(KUMUHEA is extremely tired and quickly falls asleep. He snores. WAIPUNA stays awake. She slowly nudges and slightly rocks KUMUHEA to see if he is in a deep sleep. He is out cold.*
>
> *WAIPUNA gets out of bed and puts her father's plan into action. She retrieves the rope and ties the free end to KUMUHEA's leg. WAIPUNA returns to sleep.*
>
> *KUMUHEA awakes shortly after. As the night before, he checks to see that WAIPUNA is asleep by lifting one of her extremities. She allows her arm to fall limp, pretending that she is asleep. KUMUHEA carefully leaves the bed, fixes the* kapa *and exits the home.*
>
> *KUMUHEA takes a few steps. The music starts as he begins to transform into the* 'enuhe. *He aims for the sweet potato patches. As before, the* 'enuhe *body actors appear and move toward KUMUHEA. As he moves along the stage floor he realizes that he is tied up and stuck. The* 'enuhe *body actors attempt to attach themselves to KUMUHEA. He thrashes about, letting out sounds of frustration. His leg, secured to the tree stump, hampers the proper joining of the* 'enuhe *body actors. The* 'enuhe

*body actors seem possessed and force
themselves on KUMUHEA. KUMUHEA is angry.
He is torn between his 'enuhe desires and his
human form. The music mirrors his
frustration. KUMUHEA's inability to completely
transform upsets him further. The passing of
time is shown with lights. The end of this scene
is the dawning of a new day.*

*WAIPUNA hears the commotion and runs
outside. She is shocked to see the huge half-
man, half-'enuhe thrashing through and
destroying the sweet potato patches.*

*KAWAI appears from upstage with a large
palau [a wooden club trimmed with razor
sharp shark's teeth] and approaches
KUMUHEA.)*

KAWAI: Eh Kumuhea, stop it! Enough already!

*(KUMUHEA is possessed by his kupua
personality. The 'enuhe body actors pull
KUMUHEA's body trying to release his leg. He
thrashes and grunts, thoroughly destroying the
sweet potato patches.)*

You busting up all the patches. Kumuhea, we not going
have any sweet potato. Kumuhea!

KUMUHEA: *(turning to KAWAI, his KUMUHEA personality partially
reasserts itself)* Heh? Eh Pops, howzit? You not going hurt
me, heh?

(fights the 'enuhe's anger and hunger)

KAWAI: Look, everything is all bust up!

KUMUHEA: *(the 'enuhe personality takes over)* And what? What you
going do? *(crushes another bunch of sweet potato leaves and
then devours a handful of leaves)*

KAWAI: I told you enough already!

> *(KUMUHEA lashes out at KAWAI. KAWAI then slashes KUMUHEA with his palau. KAWAI tries to sever the extended 'enuhe body [the two actors] from KUMUHEA.)*

WAIPUNA: Daddy, what you doing? No hurt him too much.

> *(KAWAI looks at WAIPUNA.)*

Never mind, never mind, I trust you Daddy. *(saddened)* Auē Kumuhea, why you lie to me for? Heh? Why you lie?

> *(KAWAI eventually cuts the large 'enuhe into little pieces. The atmosphere is chaotic. Pieces of fabric or parts of the 'enuhe body actors' costumes are scattered, representing the small 'enuhe which are created by the slicing. The actors may detach and throw the pieces. The 'enuhe body actors are finally detached from KUMUHEA's body.)*

WAIPUNA: Auē! Look all the little 'enuhe! *(amazed)* Get choke!

> *(KUMUHEA personality reasserts itself. He suddenly feels pain.)*

KUMUHEA: Ouch, stop! No make like that. Ow! Ow!

> *(KAWAI hits KUMUHEA one more time with the palau. KUMUHEA is flattened. The two 'enuhe body actors slowly crawl, very low to the ground, towards the exit doors. There are little 'enuhe everywhere. KAWAI stops, pulls back and looks at his daughter. KUMUHEA, doing the caterpillar movement, along with all of the small 'enuhe exit through the theatre doors, which should remain open for intermission.)*

KAWAI: You know Baby Girl, funny kine the *kupua. (KAWAI opens his arms to WAIPUNA.)* Come, we go. We go get you something for eat. I no like my daughter starving!

> *(WAIPUNA smiles. They exit out the open doors. Lights up. Intermission.)*

Squire Coldwell, Nara Springer, Ed Duncan, 'Āina Rapoza,
Lani-Girl Waiau.

KA PUHI A ME KA LOLI

CHARACTERS (in order of appearance):

KAPUHI—a *kupua* (shape-shifter) who lives as a *puhi* (eel) by day and a man by night

KALOLI—a *kupua* who lives as a *loli* (sea cucumber) by day and a man by night

'ANAPAU—a young woman, sister of **KILIPUE** and daughter of **KA'UPENA**

KILIPUE—a young woman, sister of **'ANAPAU** and daughter of **KA'UPENA**

KA'UPENA—father of **'ANAPAU** and **KILIPUE**, a fisherman

TIME: Traditional Hawai'i

PLACE: Ka Moku o Keawe

SETTING: The stage is rather bare.

> At center there is a rock platform for the nighttime meetings at the beach.

> To each side of this platform, there are small areas for the two couples to meet and engage one another.

> A home is required at stage left designated by a *lau hala* mat for the daily family encounters and sleeping area.

> Far stage right is the ocean from where the *kupua* come, transform, and are finally caught.

> Note: There is no emphasis on set pieces to create the environments. Lighting specifies one environment from another, creates special effects for the transformation scenes, and shows the passing of time.

SOURCE FOR MATERIAL: *Ka'ao Hawai'i*, traditional stories collected and told by Mary Kawena Pukui.

> This is a Hawaiian Creole English (HCE) play.

PROLOGUE

(An original hula is performed by KAPUHI and KALOLI. The hula foreshadows the shape shifting transformations that occur during the play. The chant speaks of these kupua, their characteristics and the upcoming story. The hula is somewhat a synopsis of the play. During the hula KAPUHI and KALOLI's hula movements take on a metamorphosis that allows the dancers to transform from their sea forms to their human form. Lights out on the dancers at the end of the hula. In silhouette, KA'UPENA is seen working on his fishing net for the last portion of the hula. Lights should fade out on him shortly after the hula is finished.)

CHANTER: 'Īloli i ka ipo o ke aumoe,
Moemoea i ka le'a a ka pō uliuli.
He uliuli ka lolina a ke kupua,
Loli mau i ka pō, 'oni'oni i ke aumoe.
'Oni ē, 'oni lā ke kupua i ka 'āina,
Ā ka 'āina ho'i ua kupua lā.
He u'i, he nōhea ke kupua i loli,
He kino kanaka, ua loli nō.
He kanaka i ka pō a ke ho'i i ke kai,
I kai he puhi,
I kai he loli,
Hehe'e wale ka 'au a ke kupua.
'A'ole nā he kanaka, he kupua nō ia.

SCENE 1

(A pool of light on a passionate couple, KAPUHI and 'ANAPAU, entangled and kissing erotically. KAPUHI moves his body in a serpent-like fashion; moving up and down the woman's body. His hands are uncontrollable, groping her. KAPUHI and 'ANAPAU excite each other equally, moving their lips and tongue passionately over each other. Each touch heightens the sensuality and eroticism of the scene. KAPUHI moves behind her, with one hand across her chest and the other in her hair, he licks the nape of her neck. 'ANAPAU arches her back with a climactic sound of pleasure. He lets her hair down.

With this sound the pool of light fades out as another pool of light slowly reveals KALOLI and KILIPUE about to make love. The mood here is completely different from that of KAPUHI and 'ANAPAU. It is sweet, gentle, calm, and romantic. KALOLI lies beside KILIPUE. He caresses her hair, down to her arm, and then tenderly holds her hand. Looking into her eyes, he kisses her hand. He brings his hand with hers near her face as they stare into each others' eyes. KALOLI and KILIPUE lean into each other and kiss. They move together as one body, as though they share a spiritual connection or union. The gentle caresses continue as sounds of ecstasy are heard from KAPUHI and 'ANAPAU who are now dimly lit. Light sighs and giggles from KALOLI and KILIPUE. The pools of light shortly fade out.

Next 'ANAPAU and KILIPUE cross to the center to meet. The stage is dimly lit as if the moon was the only source of light. [Note: a reflection of the moonlight off the ocean may be created if technically possible.] As 'ANAPAU and KILIPUE cross, they tidy themselves up; fixing their hair, adjusting their pā'ū [traditional Hawaiian skirt for women].

KILIPUE arrives first. She sits on the rock platform. She smiles, takes a deep breath bringing her hands up to her chest. She looks up at the stars as a love-struck teenager might.

'ANAPAU stumbles down to meet her sister, as she unsuccessfully tries to put her hair back up.)

'ANAPAU: *(rushed)* Sorry, sorry, sorry. I hope I not too late.

KILIPUE: *(gazing at the stars)* It's okay. *(beat)* Um. *(Notices their fishing implements which they stored near the rock. A change of attitude.)*

Yeah, let's hurry up. Maybe we been gone too long. *(She picks up their fishing implements.)*

'ANAPAU: Oh no, I no like Daddy be mad at us.

(A small pool of light bumps up on an intimidating KA'UPENA. He is still sitting, repairing his fishing net.)

KILIPUE: Let's just go.

(They begin to leave as 'ANAPAU returns to fixing her hair.)

Eh no make like no was worth it.

'ANAPAU: *(stopping KILIPUE)* What you mean?

KILIPUE: You had fun right?

(*Struggling to put the skewer through her hair to hold it together, 'ANAPAU laughs. The sisters look at each other, 'ANAPAU's hair is in slight disarray. KILIPUE hands 'ANAPAU her fishing implements. They laugh and return home.*

Lights reveal the home at SL. KA'UPENA is seen working on his fishing net. KILIPUE and 'ANAPAU slowly approach.)

'ANAPAU: (*pointing to her empty basket*) Look!

(*KILIPUE and 'ANAPAU look at the basket and then at each other. They both recognize that they have nothing to show from their late night fishing.*)

(*quietly to KILIPUE*) So what we going say?

KILIPUE: I don't know?

'ANAPAU: You the akamai one who always get out of trouble.

KA'UPENA: Aloha e nā kaikamāhine.

KILIPUE: Aloha nō e Pāpā. What you doing?

'ANAPAU: (*overlapping*) How are you Daddy? You feeling good? (*looks at KILIPUE, as if her question wasn't wise.*)

KA'UPENA: 'Ae, maika'i. So how was tonight?

(*KILIPUE and 'ANAPAU look at each other.*)

KILIPUE: Daddy, tonight no was the best.

'ANAPAU: Yeah, was real rough tonight.

KILIPUE: 'Ae, kaiko'o.

'ANAPAU: Tell me about it, the waves was crashing and pounding one after another, just hitting so hard and so intense, sometimes you no could see where was coming from, I couldn't even—

KILIPUE: *(interrupting)* 'Anapau, Daddy knows what kaiko'o is.

'ANAPAU: Sorry heh! I was just trying to explain how was, and what I felt, I mean *saw* tonight.

>   *(KILIPUE laughs looking at 'ANAPAU.)*

KA'UPENA: So no catch these past two nights?

KILIPUE: *(sassy)* 'Ae, the tide seems to be changing.

KA'UPENA: What you mean by that Honey Girl?

KILIPUE: Well . . . it seems to . . .

'ANAPAU: *(as if she's speaking to a child)* Daddy, sometimes the tide is high and we no can catch fish, but then sometimes it's good, the tide is low and it's good for us to gather stuffs.

KA'UPENA: Baby Girl, I know that! I'm one fisherman. *(pause)*

>   *(KILIPUE looks away. KA'UPENA moves toward*
>   *KILIPUE.)*

KA'UPENA: I just thought your sister was talking about something else? *(beat)* Maybe one different kine tide? *(beat)* Heh Honey Girl? So what, how's the tide? Or the current, how's the current? Pulling you in little bit? Pulling little bit, small kine? Heh? Little bit undertow maybe? Heh? *(looks at KILIPUE seriously)*

KILIPUE: *(looks at KA'UPENA)* No!

KA'UPENA: You sure? No more current? No more undertow?

KILIPUE: Dad, I never say nothing like that—

'ANAPAU: Ho man, I so-o-o tired. Time for moemoe heh Kili? *(walks over and nudges KILIPUE)* Let's go bed!

KA'UPENA: I see you girls in the morning.

>   *(KILIPUE and 'ANAPAU hug KA'UPENA good*
>   *night. As they leave for their sleeping quarters*

the light follows them, leaving KAʻUPENA dimly lit.)

ʻANAPAU: You, why you make like that for? Heh? You know Daddy, bumby he get all suspicious and hot with us? And then he not going let us go beach by ourself at night, he going make us go with da kine guys or aunty them or maybe even he going start coming with us, like we don't know what we doing or something. Ho I tell you. I wish you would just—

KILIPUE: Just shut up already. *(lies down on the mat to sleep)*

ʻANAPAU: *Me* shut up? You the one over there talking about your tide changing. Pau already, Dad going know what we stay doing every night at the beach. *(Kneels down on the mat then imitates riding a wave. Sexual innuendo with her next line.)* He probably know what kine wave you was riding this past two nights. Ho the big the wave, so rough but, oh feel so good. Only pounding one after another—

KILIPUE: You know what, I don't wanna hear it. Let's just go sleep.

(*ʻANAPAU lies down, trying to get comfortable. A long pause.)*

ʻANAPAU: You think he know anything?

KILIPUE: What you mean?

ʻANAPAU: *(rolling her eyes)* Uh come on.

KILIPUE: Probably not. Ssh! Just be quiet and go sleep.

ʻANAPAU: Alright then!

(*Light out on ʻANAPAU and KILIPUE. KAʻUPENA is dimly lit.)*

KA'UPENA: Ho my girls . . . growing up so fast. Pau swimming in the little tide pool. They ready for the big ocean, beyond the reef. Break all the rules. *(shakes his head)* They only think they ready for the big ocean. They don't even know what it's really like out there, when you start for go outside the reef. As how when you young, you don't know that the reef is there for protect us, and keep us in check. *(pause)* Pretty soon they going learn why get reef, and why we gotta respect that reef.

> *(Lights out.)*

SCENE 2

> *(The sun slowly descends.* KILIPUE *and* 'ANAPAU *wait outside of their house very eager to leave for their nightly rendezvous.* 'ANAPAU *is less successful in hiding her anxiety.*
>
> KA'UPENA *repairs a large fishing net.*
>
> KILIPUE *and* 'ANAPAU *look around. They jiggle their baskets back and forth. They mess with their* pā'ū, *their hair, and fishing implements to pass the time. It is obvious that they cannot wait much longer. They look at each other. Then look at their father. And back at each other.* 'ANAPAU *signals with her head to* KILIPUE *to ask permission to leave.* KILIPUE *refuses.* 'ANAPAU *is frustrated and signals again using larger gestures.*
>
> KA'UPENA *notices and returns to his net.*

KILIPUE signals to 'ANAPAU to ask. 'ANAPAU watches their father for a moment and hesitates.)

'ANAPAU: Okay Dad, we going.

(KA'UPENA stops his net work and looks at them.)

The sun is almost down. *(she stands)* Little more sunset, right Kili?

KILIPUE: 'Ae, *(stands)* little more sunset. We better get going.

(KA'UPENA returns to repairing the net. A long pause. KILIPUE and 'ANAPAU wait, looking back and forth at KA'UPENA and each other.)

KA'UPENA: A hui hou.

'ANAPAU and **KILIPUE:** *(leaving)* A hui hou aku nō.

(Lights out on KA'UPENA.)

(KILIPUE and 'ANAPAU cross to the rock platform.)

'ANAPAU: Right on! I never realize how long the sun take for suckin' sink down into the ocean. But that's how heh? When you waiting for something for happen, the time, he just stretch out, and seem like you waiting forever, yeah!?

(No response from KILIPUE.)

Kili, you heard what I just said or what?

KILIPUE: Uh? Yeah.

'ANAPAU: What then? What I just said?

KILIPUE: *(despondent)* Okay.

'ANAPAU: Eh Kili, you alright?

KILIPUE: Yeah I'm fine.

'ANAPAU: You sure?

KILIPUE: Yeah I sure!

'ANAPAU: You sure you sure?

KILIPUE: Yes. Why?

'ANAPAU: Just checking, kay. *(pause)* You just seem little serious as all.

KILIPUE: And what?

'ANAPAU: Nothing.

> *(A long pause as KILIPUE and 'ANAPAU place their fishing implements.)*

You sure you alright?

KILIPUE: I'm fine. It's just that all day I can not [can-na] wait for night time. I just like wake up at night and come here for meet my ipo.

'ANAPAU: Eh, I know what you mean.

KILIPUE: I no can stop thinking about him. *(Looks for KALOLI, gazes in front of her as if looking down a long beach.)*

'ANAPAU: Tell me about it. I come so happy when I see the sun coming down, cause I know it's almost time for come down over here and meet da kine, and we get to be together and it's all good and we get to da kine any kine way we like, as much as we like.

KILIPUE: Yeah I know.

'ANAPAU: Sometimes I wish the night no would end.

KILIPUE: For real! *(continues to look out toward the ocean for KALOLI.)*

'ANAPAU: Imagine if you and da kine could be together all day and all night.

KILIPUE: I wish!

ʻANAPAU: Eh Kili, you think you guys would da kine all day?

KILIPUE: *All* day?

ʻANAPAU: Yeah, *all* day!

KILIPUE: No stopping? No breaks?

ʻANAPAU: Yeah! Nah, nah, nah, gotta have breaks in between. *(beat)* For catch your breath, let the tide rise again. You know the tide, *(raising her forearm and fist as an erection)* he rise . . . to its highest peak *(shakes her arm and opens her hand as an explosion)* and then he go down again *(drops her hand limp)*. But always going get one more high tide for go again.

KILIPUE: You so funny ʻAnapau!

> *(KILIPUE and ʻANAPAU laugh.)*

ʻANAPAU: Eh you and da kine, you guys talk or what?

KILIPUE: Talk?

ʻANAPAU: Yeah. He told you anything or what?

KILIPUE: Tita [tee-ta], there's other ways for communicate.

ʻANAPAU: Yeah, you right. Why waste time talking when you can be—

KILIPUE: *(notices KALOLI and KAPUHI approach)* E, e, e. Here, they coming now!

ʻANAPAU: *(admiring KAPUHI)* Oh tita, I'm weak already.

KILIPUE: I'm in love girl!

ʻANAPAU: *(to KALOLI and KAPUHI)* Aloha mai.

> *(KALOLI and KAPUHI approach. They do not say anything to the women. They use their bodies to communicate.)*

KAPUHI is the first to move in on 'ANAPAU. He anxiously takes her hand and kisses the inner palm. He then proceeds to kiss her neck. KAPUHI and 'ANAPAU hug.

During this time KALOLI and KILIPUE stare at one another. Then slowly KALOLI approaches KILIPUE. They hug, KILIPUE puts her head on KALOLI's shoulder.

'ANAPAU and KAPUHI cling on to one another.)

'ANAPAU: *(pulls back from KAPUHI)* Real quick, kay?

(KAPUHI nods.)

(to KILIPUE) Tita, I meet you back right here.

(KILIPUE smiles and nods.)

(to KAPUHI) Okay let's go.

(KAPUHI picks 'ANAPAU up, puts her over his shoulder and exits. They should go to the same light pool as in the opening scene, which remains unlit at this time.

KALOLI and KILIPUE continue to hug.)

KILIPUE: You know I really like meeting you over here every night.

(KALOLI smiles and gently kisses her cheek.)

I wish we could be together all day, every day.

(KALOLI looks her in the eyes and pulls her close. She enjoys the closeness, taking a deep breath and sighing. He then escorts her off to their secluded area as the lights go up on KAPUHI and 'ANAPAU.

KAPUHI squats in front of 'ANAPAU who sits above him. He rustles her pāʻū up and down her thighs, she touches his face. He opens her thighs as he caresses them. She looks down at him with great anticipation and intense passion. He goes under her pāʻū and her body shivers. 'ANAPAU is estatic. After a brief period of time she has an explosive orgasm. As she climaxes the lights cross fade to KALOLI and KILIPUE.

KALOLI and KILIPUE are lying next to each other cuddling. She lies on his chest running her fingers down the center and then around the nipple area. He is ticklish. She continues giggling to herself.)

KILIPUE: I love being with you.

(KALOLI looks with agreement. They snuggle.)

I just wanna be with you forever and ever.

(Pause as she lightly kisses his chest.)

Let's sleep here and watch the sunrise.

(KALOLI lifts up and kisses her quickly. KILIPUE sits up. He stands her up, leans over and whispers in her ear.)

Me too! You sure you no can stay?

(He nods and then he exits.)

A hui hou till tomorrow night.

(KALOLI looks back, smiles, lifts his eyebrows and blows her a kiss. KILIPUE smiles and grooms herself; adjusting her hair and pāʻū.

> *'ANAPAU is seen at the same time crossing to
> the central platform. She is a little wobbly.*
>
> *'ANAPAU and KILIPUE meet. With her hands,
> 'ANAPAU is brushing her hair.)*

'ANAPAU: Girl did da kine just leave real fast?

KILIPUE: Yeah was kind of weird.

'ANAPAU: For real, no?!

> *(grabbing their baskets)*

Eh maybe we get little time for you know . . .

KILIPUE: Nah, we go home already.

'ANAPAU: Why? Maybe if we bring a little something, Daddy not
going think nothing?

KILIPUE: I don't know?

'ANAPAU: Come on, we go just try, kay?

KILIPUE: Okay shoots.

> *(KILIPUE and 'ANAPAU prepare for gathering as
> they exit.*
>
> *KA'UPENA is seen at home again with his net in
> the same position as the earlier scene. He looks
> at it. Then puts it down. He stands up goes to
> the entrance way and looks for his daughters.
> There is no sign of them.)*

KA'UPENA: *(to himself)* Where's my girls? Something inside my
na'au tells me that something is up.

> *(Voices offstage. KILIPUE and 'ANAPAU laugh.)*

(relieved) There's my girls.

> *(The light reveals KILIPUE and 'ANAPAU
> returning home.)*

Aloha e ku'u mau kaikamāhine. Pehea 'olua?

'ANAPAU: We good Daddy. How you feel?

KA'UPENA: Maika'i a'e.

'ANAPAU: Why, something was wrong earlier?

KA'UPENA: I was a little worried about you girls—

'ANAPAU: Daddy, you no need worry about us, we big girls. We can take care of ourself if anybody make trouble. *(beat)* But it's not like we see anybody when we down at the beach or anything. You know what I mean it's just me and Kilipue, we go down and do our business and then we come straight home, straight home for see you, cause we know you waiting for us, and we no like make you nervous or upset or whatever. You know heh Daddy, we care about you that's why.

> *(During the following line of questioning between KA'UPENA, KILIPUE, and 'ANAPAU, we see the transformations of both KAPUHI and KALOLI accompanied by the music in the prologue. They both slowly wade into the ocean at SR. KAPUHI transforms into an eel and KALOLI transforms into a sea cucumber. Indicate transformations with a slow body movement similar to the prologue hula. As they morph they take on the mannerisms of their sea shape. For example, KAPUHI should concentrate on the wide opening and closing of the mouth, as eels do, along with swift serpent-like movements. Light this transformation either in silhouette or back light to create a supernatural feel.)*

KA'UPENA: I know. So Honey Girl, how was things tonight? How was the tide?

'ANAPAU: Dad was little bit rough tonight. We had to go only fast kine and we never really get anything.

KA'UPENA: Fast kine? What you mean, you guys was gone all night—

'ANAPAU: A yeah but 'um—

KA'UPENA: Honey Girl what your sister trying for say?

KILIPUE: I don't know—

KA'UPENA: What you mean, you don't know? You was with her, right?

'ANAPAU: She was with me Daddy, I promise.

KA'UPENA: So what Honey Girl, you was with her or not?

KILIPUE: Yeah.

'ANAPAU: She was Daddy!

KA'UPENA: You guys not seeing anybody oceanside heh?

'ANAPAU: No, not even Dad. I told you we come straight home after we pau.

KA'UPENA: After you pau what?

'ANAPAU: What you mean?

KILIPUE: I tired, I going sleep.

KA'UPENA: Going sleep?

KILIPUE: 'Ae, we tired, we was out all night.

'ANAPAU: That's true. We tired. Me and Kili going moe, kay?

> *(A long pause. It is a very uncomfortable moment as 'ANAPAU and KILIPUE wait for KA'UPENA's approval.)*

KA'UPENA: Tired? You must be real busy oceanside, heh?

(*KILIPUE nervously looks at 'ANAPAU.*)

So what? You girls was working 'um?

'ANAPAU: Was what Daddy? Working what?

KA'UPENA: I don't know, you said you guys real tired and you gotta go moe already.

KILIPUE: Okay Dad, we tired. You know that already.

(*Pause, KA'UPENA looks at the girls.*)

KA'UPENA: Okay that's fine. You girls have a good night sleep. (*beat*) I see you in the morning.

(*KILIPUE begins to exit. 'ANAPAU gives KA'UPENA a hug. KILIPUE looks back and returns. She kisses KA'UPENA on his cheek. KILIPUE and 'ANAPAU exit.*

KA'UPENA watches them leave. Lights out.)

SCENE 3

(*Lights up on KILIPUE and 'ANAPAU sleeping, they are out cold. The sun is brightly shining; it is mid-morning.*)

KA'UPENA: (*approaches*) Hūi e ala mai, wake up. The day is almost pau, it's passing you girls by, time for wake up.

(*KILIPUE and 'ANAPAU toss a bit, but continue in their deep sleep.*)

(*moving in closer*) Come on, wake up Honey Girl. You guys miss breakfast already, pretty soon you going miss lunch too. (*beat*) Hūi e ala mai!

(*They bury their heads.*)

Some night you girls must of have. No can get up today, auē! *(exits)*

> *(KILIPUE and 'ANAPAU continue to sleep.*
>
> *KA'UPENA goes to the outside area and returns to his net, repairing the snags and minor holes. The lights should indicate the passing of the day. The passing of time should also be punctuated musically, perhaps with an* ipu *(gourd) or* kā'eke'eke *(a bamboo instrument). KA'UPENA's activity slows during the light change. He freezes once KILIPUE and 'ANAPAU start moving. KILIPUE and 'ANAPAU wake as the day comes to an end; the lights indicate the setting sun. KILIPUE and 'ANAPAU sit up and stretch. 'ANAPAU looks outside realizing they have slept the entire day.)*

'ANAPAU: Auē, we been sleeping all day from last night. Ho we must have been tired. Eh Kili, get up. Hurry up, it's just about time for us to go down to the beach and meet da kine guys.

KILIPUE: *(very sleepy)* I getting up.

> *(KILIPUE and 'ANAPAU slowly get to their feet and put their* kapa *blankets away. KILIPUE is very groggy and weak.)*

'ANAPAU: I cannot believe how long we had sleep.

KILIPUE: 'Anapau, you sure it's time for go?

'ANAPAU: 'Ae, wake up and look outside. *(moving over to KILIPUE)* Eh, you look like you saw one ghost or something.

KILIPUE: What you talking about?

'ANAPAU: Your face no more color.

KILIPUE: I just had wake up! *(looks at 'ANAPAU)* You look sick too!

ʻANAPAU: Eh cut it out! Let's go already.

> *(KILIPUE and ʻANAPAU move outside. Scurrying around they gather their baskets and fishing implements.*
>
> *KAʻUPENA loses his frozen pose. He starts to put the net away.)*

KAʻUPENA: Eh you finally when wake up. You girls wanna eat? *(beat)* You had sleep all day and never eat.

ʻANAPAU: Mahalo Dad, but we gotta get going before the sun go down.

KAʻUPENA: Nah, that's okay. Maybe you girls should stay home tonight.

KILIPUE: What?

KAʻUPENA: Maybe you should rest some more or work on some stuff over here.

> *(A long pause as KILIPUE and ʻANAPAU look at one another.)*

So what you think? You know maybe I could come and give you girls some tips—

KILIPUE: No. *(retreats)*

KAʻUPENA: What was that?

ʻANAPAU: I think, Kili like us go by ourself tonight. *(leaning over to her father)* You know heh Dad, we like talk girl kine stuff.

KAʻUPENA: Maybe Aunty can go with you girls then?

ʻANAPAU: Nah Dad, we get ʻum. We can handle.

KAʻUPENA: You sure? We can go see if Aunty busy—

ʻANAPAU: Nah, no worry, we get ʻum.

('ANAPAU signals to KILIPUE to plead with their father.)

KA'UPENA: Well I see you girls later this evening.

'ANAPAU and **KILIPUE:** 'Ae, a hui hou.

KA'UPENA: E, e, e. A hui hou.

> *(KILIPUE and 'ANAPAU exit with their baskets.*
>
> *KA'UPENA watches them leave and then quickly follows.*
>
> *KILIPUE and 'ANAPAU wander to the central platform.*
>
> *KA'UPENA continues to follow, hiding behind the boulders at the beach. He perches on a boulder and sees KAPUHI in eel form and KALOLI in sea cucumber form moving toward the seashore.)*

KA'UPENA: Ho brah, that's one pretty big puhi and how's that loli?

> *(With the same music and hula, KAPUHI and KALOLI transform from sea life into men.)*

KA'UPENA: *(to himself)* I knew it. Kupua. *(moves to better vantage point)*

> *(KAPUHI and KALOLI cross the stage to where KILIPUE and 'ANAPAU wait.)*

'ANAPAU: Ho that was close, Daddy almost never let us come. *(pause)* Eh Kili, you really think I look sick?

KILIPUE: No, I was just saying that because you said my face never have color.

'ANAPAU: You kinda look pale.

KILIPUE: Maybe because we been sleeping all day. How many days we never go in the sun now!?!

'ANAPAU: That's true.

KILIPUE: Where is my sweetheart, I need him. I have to see him.

'ANAPAU: Girl, I think you stay obsessed with him or something. You gotta control yourself.

KILIPUE: You should talk.

'ANAPAU: I not the one all mane'o and stressing about my ipo.

KILIPUE: No act 'Anapau, you just as bad as me, in fact you more worse than me!

'ANAPAU: Eh, relax over there!

KILIPUE: I think so tonight, I going ask da kine for come home with me and meet Dad.

'ANAPAU: What? You crazy or what?

KILIPUE: No, I serious. I think Dad should meet him.

'ANAPAU: Girl, you losing it! If Daddy knew what we was doing every night, he would snap!

KILIPUE: Why? How you know?

'ANAPAU: No, I know! How you going explain how you guys had meet?

KILIPUE: Listen, if me and him going be together, then he gotta meet Dad and Dad just gotta accept my—

(*KAPUHI and KALOLI approach.*)

'ANAPAU: (*excited*) Girlfriend they coming.

(*KA'UPENA watches closely. The couples meet up.*)

Here you stay.

(KAPUHI and 'ANAPAU embrace.)

I when miss you so much.

KILIPUE: I so glad you came.

(KALOLI and KILIPUE embrace. The couples freeze.)

KA'UPENA: As what I thought. My na'au was right.

(Pause. The couples kiss and then freeze.)

That's why they so tired and no like eat! The kupua sucking everything out of them. They super-tired, they no like eat, they only like come over here at night and be with the kupua. That's it! I going teach these girls one lesson. *(exits)*

(The men carry the women off to their respective love-making areas. The couples make-out and move into erotic positions. The couples freeze. Lights fade on the couples, only silhouettes of the entangled bodies remain.

KA'UPENA enters carrying his net. He walks to the ocean and methodically lays his net down to catch the kupua.

Lights completely out on the couples.

KA'UPENA hides, holding the rope to trigger the trap.

In a few seconds KAPUHI and KALOLI approach the ocean. They carefully look to see if anyone is around. After signaling to one another that the coast is clear, they plunge into the water and accompanied by music they transform.

Seeing the near complete transformation, KA'UPENA pulls the rope.

> *KAPUHI in eel form and KALOLI in sea
> cucumber form fight to get out of the net.*
>
> *KA'UPENA fights and struggles to pull them in.
> Finally, he must beat them still with a club. He
> then drags them off-stage as the lights fade out
> on him.*
>
> *By this time, KILIPUE and 'ANAPAU arrive
> home. They put down their fishing implements
> and enter the house.)*

'ANAPAU: Girl it's pretty late.

KILIPUE: *(totally exhausted)* Eh Dad must be in the front house already.

'ANAPAU: You think so?

KILIPUE: Yeah it's late already, he probably sleeping.

'ANAPAU: Yeah, you right. Sleep sounds real good.

KILIPUE: We go sleep.

'ANAPAU: You know Kili, I think, I'm in love.

KILIPUE: Girl, how you stay!?

'ANAPAU: How I stay, what about all that talk tonight about Dad just gotta accept your choice. And it's time for them to meet like that.

KILIPUE: *(half asleep)* Yeah, whatever. See you in the morning.

> *(KILIPUE and 'ANAPAU walk to their sleeping
> mats and doze off. The lights should dim
> showing the midnight hour.*
>
> *KA'UPENA is SR of the house covering an imu
> (underground oven) with banana leaves and
> mat covering. He places a few rocks on top of*

the outer edges of the mat and freezes after placing the last rock.

KILIPUE and 'ANAPAU toss and turn, having nightmares. They moan and have stomach cramps.)

'ANAPAU *(simultaneously)*: Eh. E-e . . . a-a . . . eh Kapuhi.

KILIPUE *(simultaneously)*: Auē. A-a-a . . . Kaloli ē.

(They continue to toss and moan for five to ten seconds and then freeze. Lights out.)

<u>SCENE 4</u>

(Lights up on the sleeping mat area. KILIPUE and 'ANAPAU are in a deep sleep.

Lights up on KA'UPENA removing food (the puhi *and* loli) *from the* imu. *The nearby open* imu *has had the majority of its contents removed.)*

KA'UPENA: *(shredding the* loli) Ho I tell you this is ripping me up inside. *(Takes cooked fish out of a ti-leaf wrapping and places it onto two platters. Pieces of cooked* kalo *(taro) are already on these platters.)* There we go. *(beat)* Now the girls going learn what happens when you fut around and lie to your parents. They going learn, that's for sure!

(KA'UPENA sets the platters down and crosses over to KILIPUE and 'ANAPAU. He tries to wake them up.)

KA'UPENA: Hūi e ala mai! It's time to eat. *(shakes their shoulders)* Wake up, you no wanna sleep your day away now. E ala mai!

(KILIPUE and 'ANAPAU wake slowly from their deep sleep. KA'UPENA continues to cajole them and actually assists them to sit up. KA'UPENA kneels down right in front of 'ANAPAU.)

Come on Baby Girl, let's go. *(reaching over)* You too Honey Girl. E ala mai!

KILIPUE: *(exhausted)* Why?

KA'UPENA: Because.

KILIPUE: Because what?

'ANAPAU: Oh Daddy we so-o-o tired!

KA'UPENA: Because I said that's why! It's late already. Come on, come on, come on. Let's go!

'ANAPAU: Okay we going get up.

KA'UPENA: Let's go! Let's go! You girls take forever for wake up. Too much work maybe?

(KILIPUE and 'ANAPAU slowly stumble off their mats, put up their hair and clean up.

During this time KA'UPENA returns to the food and prepares for their entrance.

KILIPUE and 'ANAPAU join KA'UPENA who offers them breakfast.)

KA'UPENA: There's plenty food, you girls eat up now.

'ANAPAU: Mahalo.

KA'UPENA: *(handing out the platters to each daughter)* Here you go Honey Girl. And this one is for my Baby Girl.

(They start eating. First they take a small bite to taste. The food is delicious. They eat.

KA'UPENA sits and watches.)

'ANAPAU: Dad you not going eat?

> *(KILIPUE and 'ANAPAU eat ravenously. The food is intoxicating.)*

KA'UPENA: No, no. I eat already before you guys had wake up.

> *(KILIPUE and 'ANAPAU nod.)*

Eat up. You girls enjoy now.

> *(In no time KILIPUE's plate is empty. Soon after 'ANAPAU finishes.)*

How was the food, 'ono?

'ANAPAU: Yeah that was 'ono! What was that, puhi?

KA'UPENA: 'Ae. And how about your's Honey Girl? 'Ono the loli?

KILIPUE: Mahalo Dad, was real 'ono.

KA'UPENA: Good, good, good. You know what girls, last night after you when leave, I just had one feeling for do some late night fishing.

> *(KILIPUE and 'ANAPAU look at each other with surprise and nervousness.)*

So anyways I when go lay net. Yeah I when lay net cause I saw one big puhi and loli. And sure enough, I had catch 'um.

> *(KILIPUE and 'ANAPAU are uncertain how to react.)*

You know, I never see you girls there at the beach.

> *(KILIPUE starts having stomach cramps. She holds her tummy. The sisters fear their secret is no longer a secret.)*

Maybe we just had miss each other, yeah? But anyway, getting back to the puhi and loli. You know they no

usually come that big. Ho I tell you, real different this
kine.

> *(An ache starts in the sisters' stomachs.*
> *Nevertheless they listen to KA'UPENA.)*

Anyways the puhi and the loli you when just eat . . . The
ones I had catch last night . . .

> *(During the following dialogue, the sisters*
> *become more sick, their bellies aching until*
> *they feel the urge to vomit. They are disgusted*
> *by the following revelation from their father.)*

I hope you when enjoy 'um, because well I when hand
pick 'um for you girls. I think you know them already.
You know, the handsome mens you girls been visiting
with every night, the ones who been distract you from
fishing and who made you girls lie to me, your Daddy.
Yep, you know your guys lovers from the nightly
rendezvous on the beach, they kupua, the kine I been
warn you about, but no, you guys no like listen, you
think you guys know everything heh? You think you
guys big already, can fool your Daddy . . . NO! I no think
so! No can, no way, no how, cause I know I'm your guys
Daddy. I know this kine stuffs!

KILIPUE: I feel sick.

'ANAPAU: Even me, I sick.

KA'UPENA: You sick?

> *(KA'UPENA pick up his club.)*

KILIPUE: I think I going puke—

'ANAPAU: Even me, I going puke.

KA'UPENA: You going puke?

KILIPUE : My stomach sore!

'ANAPAU: Even me, sore my stomach!

KA'UPENA: Sore stomach?

> *(KILIPUE and 'ANAPAU heave and shortly after vomit in an extremely exaggerated and stylized way.*
>
> *KAPUHI and KALOLI, in their sea life forms, appear behind 'ANAPAU and KILIPUE and gesture with their arms as if a miniature eel and sea cucumber are expelled from mouths of women. KILIPUE and 'ANAPAU are in shock and scream. They are nauseated and repulsed by the sight of KAPUHI and KALOLI in their sea life forms squirming in front of them.*
>
> *KAPUHI and KALOLI flop around and try to run away toward the ocean.*
>
> *KA'UPENA has his club prepared and chases after them, beating them with his club.*
>
> *KALOLI is taken out with a few hits. He lies flat on the ground.*
>
> *KILIPUE and 'ANAPAU retreat from the action holding one another. Their expressions are of regret and disbelief.*
>
> *KAPUHI is much more feisty and seems to have an opportunity to escape.*
>
> *KA'UPENA is prepared, he takes out his* newa *[war club]. He jumps on KAPUHI and lunges slicing KAPUHI's neck.*
>
> *All freeze. Lights out.)*

SCENE 5

(KA'UPENA at center stage. The very bright sun indicates the dry, hot leeward side of the island. He carries an ipu [gourd] filled with the ashes of KAPUHI and KALOLI. He ritualistic scatters the ashes.)

KA'UPENA: The kupua in this ipu is ashes, they pau. Never again to roam on this 'āina, pau. Main thing the water no touch them, bumbye they join up again and live one more time. Pau. *(scatters the last of the ash on each line.)* No more puhi, no more loli. *(caps the ipu.)* Ua pau! *(freezes)*

(For the closing tableau; the lights dim, KA'UPENA returns to his home and sits with his fishing hooks.

KILIPUE and 'ANAPAU return home carrying baskets filled with gifts from the sea. They walk toward KA'UPENA. All make eye contact. Balance has been restored in their lives. KILIPUE and 'ANAPAU offer their baskets to KA'UPENA who smiles. They all freeze. Lights out. Ua pau!)

Tammy Haili'ōpua Baker is from Kapa'a, Kaua'i and holds a BA and an MFA in Theatre from the University of Hawai'i at Mānoa. She has directed numerous plays at Kennedy Theatre at UHM as well as with her own Hawaiian language theatre company, Kā Hālau Hanakeaka. Her MFA thesis play, *Māuiakamalo: Ka ho'okala kupua o ka moku*, written completely in Hawaiian, toured Hawaiian language immersion schools across the state in 1998 and subsequently travelled to the Pacific Arts Festival in Noumea, New Caledonia. She is an instructor in the Hawaiian and Indo-Pacific Languages and Literatures Department at UHM.

KUMU KAHUA THEATRE PRESENTS
THE RETURN OF

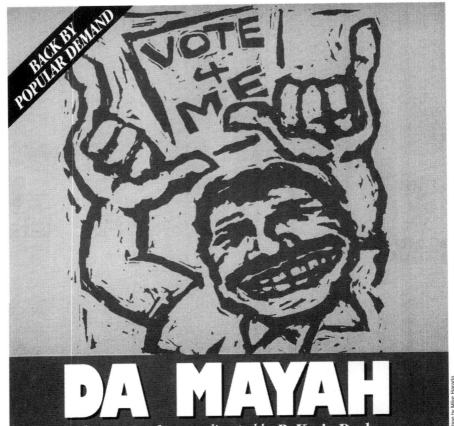

BACK BY POPULAR DEMAND

Illustration by Mike Harada

DA MAYAH
by **Lee Cataluna** • *directed by* **R. Kevin Doyle**

Those crazy characters are back! – Don't miss them this time around!

"imaginative...local comic masterpiece...well worth seeing twice..." **Honolulu Star-Bulletin**
"awfully funny...bright new voice for Kumu Kahua..." **Honolulu Advertiser**

8:00 pm: June 24, 25, 26; July 1, 2, 3, 8, 9, 10, 15, 16, 17, 1999
2:00 pm: Sundays, June 27; July 11, 18, 1999

ADMISSION:
Fridays, Saturdays and Sundays: $15 General, $12 Seniors and
Groups of 10 or more, $10 Students
Thursdays: $12 General, $10 Seniors & Unemployed, $5 Students

KUMU KAHUA
THEATRE
46 Merchant Street
(Corner of Merchant and Bethel)

BOX OFFICE: 536-4441
Box Office and Phone Line open
Monday through Friday 11:00AM – 3:00PM

Public parking for performances is available in the
Harbor Court Building, across the street from the theatre.

Kumu Kahua productions are supported
by the State Foundation on Culture and
the Arts through appropriations from the
Legislature of the State of Hawai'i,
celebrating more than thirty years
of culture and the arts in Hawai'i;
the Mayor's Office of Culture and Arts,
Jeremy Harris, Mayor; The Hawaii Community
Foundation and Foundations,
Businesses and Patrons.

Da Mayah:
Capturing the Essence
M. Desha

Lee Cataluna is, arguably, one of Hawaiʻi's most well-known writers. The former newscaster, who has also dabbled in stand-up comedy, is currently a popular columnist for *The Honolulu Advertiser* and the most prolific local playwright in recent history.

Da Mayah was not only her first play, it was her first attempt at play writing. *Da Mayah* grew out of an assignment from Kumu Kahua's 1997 play writing class, taught by Victoria Nalani Kneubuhl: "The whole premise was an assignment on exposition. Vicky gave us five scenarios, and one of them was, 'Lester Perez, mayor of Hilo county, has a secret to keep, and he tells his secretary.' I wrote a scene for that week, the next week, I wrote the next scene, then everyone wanted to see what happened next. So, six weeks later, I had a first draft."

It was Chris Miyasato, who directed the first staged reading, who first called the play a political satire. Cataluna remembers, "I was proud and shocked. I'm glad I hadn't set out to write one, otherwise I'd have blown it."

Directed by R. Kevin Doyle, *Da Mayah* was produced in the 1997–98 season. In production, the play struck a chord with audiences, and audience members included not a few politicians. "Mufi Hannemann, Neil Abercrombie, John Waihee—and Mufi's staff came back on their own a couple of other nights," Cataluna remembers. Two characters added during production—stereotypical county workers—drove home criticisms about government and service. "I don't know if I could have written about these things in a non-comedic way without being heavy handed. Personally, I wouldn't have been interested."

"I don't think the comedy softened the blows: it allowed the punches to land," Doyle notes. "People generally don't like it when you preach at them. They don't handle criticism well—they shut off. Humor opens the window—her comedy lets the truth be seen."

Despite the subject matter, Cataluna feels the reason *Da Mayah* was so popular wasn't because of the political commentary. "Even though it's called *Da Mayah*, it's Sandra's play. Her ambition, that she channeled to someone who wasn't worth it. It was about her coming into her own."

Toward that end, Doyle and the cast did a lot of status-related exercises with the characters, examining how people of higher and lower status related to each other, e.g., an employer-employee relationship.

"There's a speech that Sandra gives, about the old days," Cataluna notes. "She speaks of a fondness for a simple time when people were nicer, motives weren't suspect. One where stopping at Aunty's house for *pão doce* is a reasonable excuse for being late to work."

"That simplicity and sense of family is the Hawaiian heart of the play," she says. "They don't talk about progress, they talk about the virtues of a simpler time."

As a journalist and playwright Cataluna calls attention to both the good and bad, to illustrate "a uniquely Hawai'i story," she says. "I think as a part of growing up here, you learn that you can't pick on anyone littler than you. I'm not making fun of a specific bad boss—and everyone's had one—but the thing is, the boss always has more power than you. He's bigger.

"In the *Advertiser*, I like to write about the little guys succeeding with dignity. Within the context of the play, it's Sandra realizing she's not a 'little guy.' The current mayor hurts the people of Hilo—so he's fair game."

"My work is influenced by my job. I write about today," Cataluna says. "It isn't meant to be timeless."

Doyle disagrees, likening Cataluna's writing to classic satirists, such as Aristophanes. "I think that if you took away all the contemporary references, you'd still have a very funny play. The wonderful part is not the jokes, it's the way she captures the characters—they're real."

"They say the best playwrights are former actors and former journalists, and Lee is both," says Doyle. "Lee know what people are like. She can capture a person onstage in ten lines. It's a rare gift."

Sherry Clifton, Eddy Gudoy.

DA MAYAH

BY

LEE CATALUNA

Da Mayah was first produced by Kumu Kahua Theatre in Honolulu on September 5, 1998. The production was directed by R. Kevin Doyle with the following cast:

LESTER PEREZ . . . . .Eddy Gudoy
SANDRALENE FERREIRA . . . . .Sherry Clifton
DUKIE . . . . .BullDog
STANTON . . . . .Daryl Bonilla
JAZZMIN . . . . .Ly Atsumi
BIG AL . . . . .Stu Hirayama

Set Design: BullDog
Light Design: Gerald Kawaoka
Costume Design: Lisa Ann M. Omoto
Sound Design: Keith K. Kashiwada
Backdrop Design: Corky Trinidad
Cheesy Karaoke Music Composition: Roslyn Cattracchia
Cheesy Karaoke Music Arrangement: David Kauahikaua
Assistant Director/Stage Manager: Rolinda Emch

ACT I

SCENE 1

*(LESTER stands at a podium in a spotlight.
There are campaign signs and streamers behind
him, and microphones on the podium. The
signs read "Perez for Mayor" and "Lester
Perez—Do What He Sez!" A crowd can be
heard cheering. LESTER wears many leis.)*

LESTER: Ladies and gentlemen, and you in-between types from
brother Rocky Auwai's hula halau, I stand before you
tonight a victorious victor after a hard won victory. It is
my supreme honor to have been elected as Hilo's first
mayor. And as your new mayor, I promise, we going beat
Kona County in every intra-mural government workers
horseshoe tournament, even if I have to shoe the horses
myself.

As a famous guy once said, "I have not yet begun to
fight . . . I going wait for my backers to show up." And
ladies and gentlemen, YOU are my backers!

For many years, the Big Island has been facing a de Lima.

SANDRA: *(Yelling from offstage)* That's dilemma!

LESTER: Dilemma. Should we attempt to stay together, east side
and west side, as one huge county, or split apart into
sister counties, working together but separately on
common but completely unrelated goals. I am proud yet
boastful to have been chosen the first mayor to lead Hilo
into the new millinimum.

SANDRA: *(vo)* Millennium!

LESTER: Millinimum. Millimanum. Whatever.

The business community in this town has been sufferating, and I intend to change that. Hilo will welcome all new en-TREP-aners

SANDRA: *(vo)* Entrepreneurs!

LESTER: Whatever—to set up shop on our shores . . . but not too close to the shores because a tidal wave could come and buss everything up again. Then we'd really be screwed.

SANDRA: *(vo)* Stick to the script!

LESTER: As your new mayor, I want you, the little people of Hilo, to know that the door to my office is always opened to you—except when I'm not there. I gotta keep it locked because the crime in this town is horrible and I'm pretty sure that koa desk in there is worth something.

In conclusion, I am so grateful yet consternated that you came to your senses and elected me as your leader over that loser from Wainaku. For a while there, I thought that guy was paying you guys off more than I was and I thought "impossible!" But in the end, you came through for Lester Perez, and I promise you, you won't live to regret it!

SCENE 2

(The mayor's office)

SANDRA: *(rushing in through the office door)* Sorry sorry sorry Mistah Mayah! I know I late but I jess wen go down to pick up one plate lunch from Sun Sun Lau—cause you know, Thursdays they get their Reduced Fat tripe stew—but then I forgot was Wednesday, so I had to drive all the way back to Dotty's and . . . Ay, Mistah Mayah. What had happen to you? You look like you seen a ghost or something.

LESTER: No.

SANDRA: You nevah eat the pastele plate special from Tina Tunta's Lunch Wagon again, ah? I told you no buy from her. She get her pork cheap from her uncle's pig farm cause all the hogs got mad cow disease.

LESTER: Sandralene, I may want to cancel my meetings for this afternoon.

SANDRA: Ay ke Jesus. Dis is serious.

LESTER: Who's on my calendar?

SANDRA: Well, there's Legs Yokotake at two, and it says, parentheses, campaigned for you in Papaikou and wants a job. There's Roachy Kalima at two-thirty . . . campaigned for you in Hakalau and wants a job. At three, there's a Mister Kingsford Pavao. It says he put your bumper sticker on top his horse trailer, and now he wants a job. And then at three-thirty, Na Keiki O Busy Hands Pre-School are going to stage a protest in your office for make you stop desecrating the ʻāina. Oh, and they want a tour of the council chambers.

LESTER: Yeah. Cancel them all.

SANDRA: 'Kay. *(pause)* That's funny.

LESTER: What?

SANDRA: I don't see Derek Pang's name in here.

LESTER: You know Derek Pang?!

SANDRA: Shuah! Him and my third husband got to be good friends when they was serving time together in O-triple-C. I used to fly to Honolulu once a month for visit and bring them banana bread. Good, you know. With nuts.

And those Hilo boys, they got to be real close on the inside. Oh! But not that kind close, if you know what I mean.

LESTER: Sandra . . .

SANDRA: I seen him outside walking across the parking lot wearing his *Men In Black* sunglasses.

LESTER: You sure was him?

SANDRA: I would reckanotice that buss-up face anywhere! Besides, no too many six-foot five, muscle-head Chinese dudes walking around Hilo. In fact, I seen him just last Saturday night at Jazzmin's Karaoke Bar and Washerette. You know, bradda Derek can sing dat karaoke. He could go Hawai'i Stars and blow Carole Kai's doors.

LESTER: *(aside)* He's going to blow my doors if I don't think of something fast.

SANDRA: So yeah, I know Derek Pang pretty good. *(slows down for once. Slyly.)* Da question is, how YOU know him. Not like you guys would hang out together in the Hilo Yacht Club, if you catch my drifts.

LESTER: We were, uh, childhood friends.

SANDRA: No kidding! What, Saint Joe's class of 1962? Small world!

LESTER: *(sighs)* Too small.

SANDRA: Hey, you really upset no, Mistah Mayah? Here I am trying to be my happy, bubbly self that you love so much and you just bringing me down like one bad batch of lomi salmon.

LESTER: He wants a job.

SANDRA: A job! Like he's qualified to work for you! Make him county dog catcher!

LESTER: I thought of that. I'm afraid he'd go around shooting all the dogs.

SANDRA: No kidding. What he get on you anyway? I know he nevah campaign for you because his name not on my list of people we gotta be nice to. And I know he nevah give you money cause his name not on my list of people we gotta be really really nice to. So what! *(whining)*

LESTER: It happened a long time ago.

SANDRA: Mistah Mayah . . . *(looks around to see if anyone is within earshot)* Lester, Les Baby *(caressing LESTER)* You know you going feel soooo much better if you tell me.

LESTER: *(eyes closed, savoring the moment)* Yes, Sandra.

SANDRA: *(whacks LESTER on the back of the head)* So tell me!

LESTER: Yes, Sandra! You know Lawton Pacheco?

SANDRA: You mean Puka Head Pacheco?

LESTER: That's the one. You know how he got his name?

SANDRA: Somebody wen puka his head.

LESTER: It was a bungled robbery attempt, Sandra. Derek and I only wanted a couple of six-packs of Oly to take to the All-Saints Day Dance.

SANDRA: Ay ke Jesus! YOU shot Puka Head Pacheco?!

LESTER: Are you shocked?

SANDRA: I'm kind of excited.

LESTER: If this story gets out, my political career will be ruined!

SANDRA: Oh come on now. Bill Clinton smoked some kolos. That neva ruin his career. Milton Holt—oh, wait. Bad example. For crying out loud, everybody found out that Jeremy Harris's wife is not Filipino, and that nevah ruin his career!

LESTER: Ramona's not Filipino? No ways! *(beat)* Sandra, this is different. This is armed robbery and attempted murder. It can't get out.

SANDRA: I tell you what. I going call my cousin Dukie. He'll take care of Derek.

LESTER: Oh God, Sandra. Not the syndicate! Please!

SANDRA: Okay.

LESTER: Please! Please! Promise you won't!

SANDRA: All right, all right all right already.

LESTER: I'll handle this one on my own. Okay? I'm just going to go in my office and lie down for a bit. Think things over.

SANDRA: Okay, you go lie down. I'll be right in.

> *(LESTER exits, closing the door. SANDRA already is punching in the telephone number.)*

Dukie, this is Cousin Sandra. I need your assistance with a small matter for the mayah.

SCENE 3

> *(Inside Jazzmin's Karaoke Bar and Washerette. There is one table with two chairs. A sign on the wall lists prices: "Karaoke solo $1.50, duet $4.00, Anything by Air Supply $6.00, Wash 50 cents, Dry 75 cents, Fold $1.50. Soap Extra." There is a karaoke machine against the back wall. DUKIE sits at the table with a drink. A ceiling fan moves slowly overhead.)*

SANDRA: *(rushes in)* Dukie! Ay, cousin. *(kisses his cheek)* I sorry I late. I hope you no was waiting too long. Had one sale on Hinode twenty pounds at KTA and I got stuck in one long line. Was worth it, though, 'cause I picked up six bags. How you?

DUKIE: Fine, fine, Sandralene. And you looking good yourself.

SANDRA: Oh, thanks, yeah! You know, I was getting a little thick in places where I never even used to have places, if you know what I mean. So I wen switch from Best Foods to Miracle Whip in my mac salad, and from Bud to Coors lite, and in two weeks, I wen drop ten pounds. Amazing, yeah?! I should write one book like Oprah. But you looking pretty good yourself. That beard hides the place where Butchie Kitagawa wen crack you wid dat bat. And I took notice your jade ring hide da sewing scar where they wen reattach your finger.

DUKIE: The hazards of the job.

SANDRA: And how's your *(lowers her eyes)* dakine?

DUKIE: Better. Better. Thanks for asking. Sometimes I still pass some shrapnel when I'm, uh, using it. But everything is working as it should be.

SANDRA: Ay, thank God. You never found out who hid dat pipe bomb in the toilet?

DUKIE: No, Sandralene. Just a senseless act of violence. The streets of this town just not safe anymore for the decent citizens like you and me.

SANDRA: *(leans in)* I heard rumors was Junior Ugalino's people.

DUKIE: We may never know, Sandra. Junior Ugalino had an unfortunate accident yesterday and he may never come out of the coma for answer any questions.

SANDRA: What! I neva hear about dis! And I usually hear about EVERYTHING . . . sometimes even before stuff happens.

DUKIE: It was tragic, really. His son, Junior Ugalino Junior, found him. He was fixing fence up on the other son's ranch—Junior Ugalino the Third—when someone turned on da juice. Weird, you know. Somehow, the power in the line made the fence wire wrap around his body from his feet all the way up to his neck. About fifty times. There was knots, too. Square knots. Some people saying maybe was a power spike from Puna Geothermal . . . but me, I don't like to point fingers.

SANDRA: Especially since you only get nine and a half left.

DUKIE: *(snaps)* Dat's not funny!

SANDRA: Sorry, Dukie, sorry. Take it easy. You know me, always trying to keep it light and happy. *(proudly)* I wasn't voted Miss Big Big Island Aloha Spirit Congeniality Second Runner-up for nothing, you know.

DUKIE: I *did* have a hand in that.

SANDRA: Oh no. No you didn't. Maybe you get your hands in everything else in this town from Senior Citizen Bingo night to the turkey raffle at Saint Joseph's carnival every Thanksgiving, but I won that title fair and square. I earned it, just like I earned everything else in my life—the hard way.

DUKIE: Fine, Sandra. Sure.

SANDRA: The only reason I neva get Miss Big Big Island Aloha Spirit Congeniality *first* runner-up was 'cause that fricken kiss-ass Raenette Dutro was volunteering to hem everybody's dresses, haku their leis and sell their extra benefit chili tickets.

DUKIE: Sandra. Leave it alone. That's in the past. You came here to ask me something. You need my help.

SANDRA: It's not for me. It's for da mayah. Dat hoodlum Derek Pang is trowing him heat.

DUKIE: Derek get dirt on Lester Perez?

SANDRA: More dirt than one Panaewa dump truck could hold. Check this out. When Lester was 17, he—

DUKIE: *(interrupts)* I don't need to know the details. I just need to know why you're involved. I'll do nothing for Lester Perez. But you, you're blood.

SANDRA: He's da *mayah*, Dukie. I no like see him go down. Besides, would be make-ass for me. Like they say, da shit no fall too far from the donkey. And I like my job with my long lunches and greeting dignitaries and wearing power muumuus from Puamana Crabbe every day.

DUKIE: Listen to you talk. You made Lester Perez. That man couldn't even find his goddamn polling place on election day if wasn't for you. You had to drive him to the Hakalau cafeteria, for crying out loud. And then, you had to give him the full remedial voting one-oh-one lesson on how to line up his ballots in da little machine so the pukas all straight. Bradda probably couldn't even figure out how for vote for himself. You're the one running that office. You should be mayor.

SANDRA: You think I haven't thought of that? You think I haven't looked at myself in the mirror on the ceiling above my bed a thousand times and said "Sandralene Leialoha Ferreira, you got da brains, you got da guts, you got dat winning smile now that Dr. Okazaki fixed your partial. *You* should be mayah.

DUKIE: You would be a great mayor.

SANDRA: You damn straight I would be one great mayah. I know it. You know it. But the big problem is, the voters out there, they don't know it. And if I tried to tell them, they no would believe it. You think they going elect one middle-age Portuguese-Hawaiian-Albanian, five-time-married, former women's wrestling promoter and part-time plus-size swimsuit model fo be mayah? Crazy!

DUKIE: Stranger things have happened. Look at Mufi Hannemann. Sandra, you gotta follow your dreams.

SANDRA: *(serious and subdued for a moment)* I know. I will. And I am. But I need your help with this one. I need your help to get Derek Pang out of the picture.

DUKIE: For you, cousin, for you anything. I'll talk to my boys. Consider it already taken care of.

SANDRA: *(gets up, kisses DUKIE on the cheek)* Cousin, you da best! *(exits)*

SCENE 4

(Inside Jazzmin's, moments after SANDRA exits.)

DUKIE: Stanton! Get in here!

STANTON: *(rushes in from the back room. Stands almost at attention before DUKIE)* Yes, boss!

DUKIE: What do you have there in your pocket, boy?

STANTON: Oh! I keep forgetting to return this to you. It's the stuff from the last job. Wire cutter. Electrical tape. And one butter knife.

DUKIE: You can keep the butter knife.

STANTON: Thanks!

DUKIE: A little present for a job well done.

STANTON: Sheesh. Das' all I get? One butter knife?

DUKIE: Don't be stupid, now. You know you're always well taken care of.

STANTON: *(sulking)* Yes, boss.

DUKIE: Who bought you a brand new Glock when you had to ditch yours in Hilo harbor?

STANTON: You, boss.

DUKIE: And who paid for your reconstructive surgery after your unfortunate run-in with Miss Rhondalyn Contrades, who was in actuality Mister Ronald Contrades?

STANTON: You, boss.

DUKIE: And who paid off the entire jury plus alternates to get you off that quadruple homicide charge?

STANTON: Hey, that was *your* hit!

DUKIE: That's beside the point. My point is, I've always treated you like a son.

STANTON: If that's how you would treat your son, lucky thing you cannot have kids.

DUKIE: What the *hell* are you talking about?

STANTON: *(teasing)* I heard you shooting blanks.

DUKIE: That's not true!

STANTON: *(cracking up)* I don't know. I heard you used to be shooting blanks, but ever since that pipe bomb exploded when your pants was down, now you shooting bullets!

DUKIE: I'll show you pipe bombs and bullets, boy!

STANTON: I'm just playing with you, boss. Sheesh, cannot take a joke or what? You know I'm your main man. Dukie's main man. Stan da man, they call me. Stanton da manton.

DUKIE: Straighten up, boy! I got a job for you!

STANTON: 'Kay! Who you like me bump off *now*?

DUKIE: Shhhh!

STANTON: Sorry. So who's the unfortunate dude about to set up permanent residence at Pū ʻāinakō cemetery?

DUKIE: Derek Pang.

STANTON: Derek Pang! You gotta be fricken kidding! You mean that six-foot-five muscle-head Chinese dude with the buss up face? THAT Derek Pang?!

DUKIE: Is there a problem?

STANTON: Yeah, get one problem. The guys is a monstah! He's huge! Bradda can use coconut trees for one back scratcher! He can use telephone poles for toothpick. Shoot, he go Honolulu and Aloha Airlines gotta fly him over in cargo.

DUKIE: Size isn't everything.

STANTON: Spoken like a man in denial. Derek Pang is the meanest dude Hilo ever seen. He's like all ten Sua brothers rolled into one. The Hurricane Tracking Center get monitors at his house so when he get pissed off, they can send out a Pacific-wide warning. Harry Kim and Civil Defense conduct Derek Pang drills once a month. I'm telling you, he's like da Unholy.

DUKIE: It's for Sandralene. She needs the job done.

STANTON: *(stops cold)* Sandra! Why didn't you say so in the first place. *(dreamily)* I'd do anything for Sandra.

DUKIE: So now there's no problem?

STANTON: No problem at all. If Sandra needs me, I'd go to the ends of the Big Island for her. I no care if I gotta climb Mauna Loa barefoot on a winter night with nothing but

Saloon Pilot crackers to sustain me. I'd do it. Anything for her.

DUKIE: Don't get any stupid ideas about my cousin, now. You're not her type.

STANTON: Oh, and Mayor Lester Perez is? I know what's going on. I have my sources. And my sources get their sources. And those sources report to the other sources, and the sources . . . *(He gets confused. A beat to untangle himself)* I know how he treats her, and its just not right.

DUKIE: I know.

STANTON: She even had to cover for him at that big groundbreaking last week. They gave him the shovel for turn the dirt, and bradda wen use the wrong end.

DUKIE: Lester is an idiot. And Sandra is a fool for sticking by him. But she's always been that way—loving the wrong men for the wrong reasons.

STANTON: That's why she needs me. I'd be good to her. I'd be her Prince Charming. I'd treat her like the Queen-size Princess she is. She needs a good man like me.

DUKIE: You! A good man! Hah!

STANTON: Why?

DUKIE: Well, let's see. You've been a regular guest in every prison between Kulani and Sing Sing. You've got a rap sheet thicker than the Bible. In school, your home room was the principal's office. And, oh yeah, you're a mass murderer.

STANTON: So, that's just on the outside. It's what's on the inside that counts.

DUKIE: Well, whatever you need to tell yourself to keep yourself going. Just get this one done, quick. Sandra is counting on you.

STANTON: Yes, boss. Any special requests? An electrocution? A drowning? Ooh! Hilo hasn't had a good beheading in a while!

DUKIE: You take your pick. Just get it done.

STANTON: Right, boss.

(bells chiming offstage)

DUKIE: Hey, is that Tina Tunta's Pastele Wagon? Go run out there and get me the gandule rice special.

STANTON: Boss, you better not eat that crap. It'll kill you. Sandra says Tina Tunta get her pork cheap from her uncle's pig farm 'cause da pigs all get swine flu.

DUKIE: That's just a rumor. Like the rumor about Wing Ding Chop Suey and the cats. Now shut up and go. And bring me back the number six special.

(STANTON exits, shaking his head.)

SCENE 5

(mayor's office, next morning)

SANDRA: *(enters)* Sorry, sorry, sorry Mistah Mayah! I know I late. I just wen stop by Ken's Pancake house for a cup of coffee on the go, but they had the hamburger steak, fried rice and eggs short-stack combo special, and I just couldn't resist.

LESTER: That's fine, Sandra.

SANDRA: You looking like you feeling better. How's your little problem?

LESTER: Oh, fine. The swelling has gone down and it doesn't burn anymore when I . . .

SANDRA: Not *that* problem! The Derek Pang problem!

LESTER: Oh! That! Well, I've got that under control.

SANDRA: How?

LESTER: I'm going to put him on the staff.

SANDRA: What?!

LESTER: I have the perfect position lined up for him.

SANDRA: No such thing as Official County Moke.

LESTER: Oh, That's a good one. Maybe I could request funds for that position from the county council.

SANDRA: Come on now. Be serious. What position are you offering him? Not Head of Solid Waste, although that may be appropriate.

LESTER: No.

SANDRA: Not Head of Environmental Contamination?

LESTER: No.

SANDRA: Not Director of Pre-School Summer Fun . . . please!

LESTER: Nope.

SANDRA: That leaves . . . my job?!

LESTER: I thought of that. But it doesn't pay enough.

SANDRA: No kidding.

LESTER: I'm going to make Derek Pang my Director of County Protocol.

SANDRA: What! Mistah Mayah! That's too much even from you! What does Derek Pang know about protocol and proper procedures?

LESTER: What does anyone in this town know about protocol and proper procedures? This is Hilo, for crying out loud. Besides, the job will keep him quiet.

SANDRA: How quiet?

LESTER: One hundred and twenty thousand dollars a year quiet.

SANDRA: For that, even *I* could keep quiet. But Mistah Mayah, remember when we worked on the budget? We decided not to fund that position. We decided it would not be one prudent use of the taxpayers' money. Remember? There's no funding for the position.

LESTER: There is now.

SANDRA: Oh no. You didn't. Tell me you didn't.

LESTER: I did.

SANDRA: You couldn't.

LESTER: I could.

SANDRA: You mean . . .

LESTER: Yes.

SANDRA: Ay ke Jesus. You made one decision without talking to me first!

LESTER: After all, I am the mayor.

SANDRA: What did you do, Mistah Mayah!

LESTER: Nothing.

SANDRA: Lester! *(whacks him on the back of the head)* Lester, what did you do?!

LESTER: *(rubbing his head)* Ow! I hate it when you do that. It rattles my fillings. You're going to give me brain damage.

SANDRA: No can. You gotta have one brain first. Now spill it. How are you funding the Director of Protocol position?

LESTER: I took the money out of some other programs.

SANDRA: Ay, my God. Which programs, Lester?

LESTER: *(confused)* Just a couple little small programs. Nothing anyone would notice.

SANDRA: Which programs, Lester!

LESTER: Just, you know, some of the small ones.

SANDRA: Which programs? Think! Think!

LESTER: Well, I closed the Humane Society Healthy Puppy–Healthy Kitty fund. . . .

SANDRA: No!

LESTER: I cut the Senior Citizens Handi-Van transportation program. You know, let those old geezers learn how to drive like everybody else.

SANDRA: Ay, my God.

LESTER: The bulky-item and dead animal pick up program . . . oh yeah, one more. The Pana'ewa Fire Station.

SANDRA: What about it?

LESTER: Closed.

SANDRA: My god, Lester. You talking political suicide here. Derek no gotta threaten to kill you now. You saving him the trouble.

LESTER: Don't be so dramatic. No one will ever notice those programs are gone.

SANDRA: God, how am I supposed to fix this one up! Mistah Mayah, you know you have always trusted me to give you good advice. I've been your Dear Abby. Your Miss Manners. Your Ask Heloise. I've been your own personal Coast Guard as you drift around lost on the 'Alenuihāhā

Channel of your political career. And I'm telling you, do not do this. You're making a humongous mistake.

LESTER: It's my mistake to make. After all, I am the mayor. I can hire who I like and I can fire who I like. For instance, I hired you, and I can fire you. You're forgetting how you got into this office. It was me. I brought you here. And I know you think what you do is vitally important. But face it, all you do is take ridiculously long lunches, answer a few phone calls, and decide whether you're going to wear a pakalana or a pīkake lei to the Governor's reception. You must remember who I am. You must remember where I came from. I am a highly intelligent and accomplished man. Think of my background. I hold a certificate of completion from U.H. Hilo Special Learners Summer Session. I graduated with perfect attendance from Saint Joseph High School. For crying out loud, I was named Ideal Boy for the Keywanettes Club in my sophomore year. I am The Man in this town, and don't you forget it. My word is the law. So that's the way its going to be. Derek Pang is the new County Director of Protocol. And by the way, he'll need some room to work, so I'm giving him your desk. There's a desk you can use out in the other room with the rest of the clerks and stuff. You can move your things there next week.

SANDRA: But I'm not a clerk. I'm your administrative assistant. I'm second in command. If you die in office, I would be mayor.

LESTER: Quit whining. It's the nicest desk out there. It's closest to the lunch room. You'll like that. I'm going into my office to lie down. Why don't you come in and join me and we'll go into executive session. *(wiggles his eyebrows lasciviously)*

SANDRA: Yeah. Sure. I'll be right there. I just gotta take care of something first.

(*LESTER goes into his inner office and closes the door behind him.*)

SANDRA: (*to herself*) Move my desk, move my desk. Yeah, I'll move my desk. But it won't be down the hall. It'll be into that office. (*points at mayor's closed door*)

<u>SCENE 6</u>

(*Stage is bare except for a few branches or bushes*

STANTON enters, creeping on the floor like a soldier in the jungle. He is wearing camouflage pants, a black shirt, black boots, and a ski cap. As he crawls across the stage to the small clump of bushes, he unrolls a cable behind him. He is trying to be very stealthy, and frequently makes furtive glances around the stage. Though he is moving with great care, he makes a great deal of noise when his boots squeak on the stage, his tool belt jingles, and his pager goes off. Once he gets behind the bushes, he stands, still crouching a bit. He pulls out of his pocket a small electrical-type box with a red button on top.)

STANTON: Okay. Watch says three forty-five. That means Derek Pang wen sing his last karaoke song at Jazzmin's at three. G-27, "Love to Love You, Baby", which is six minutes, forty-five seconds. Five minutes for say good-bye to Jazzmin-dem. Four minutes for pick up his laundry. Thirty seconds for find his keys. Three minutes for find his car in the parking lot. Two more minutes fo get that junkalunka started. Then drive over this side. That means he should be driving over the Wailuku Bridge right about . . . *(very long pause)* NOW!

> *(STANTON presses the red button on the small box. There is a flash of light and the sound of a huge explosion.)*

Woo-hoo! I got 'em! *(runs off the stage)*

SCENE 7

(Jazzmin's. DUKIE sits at the table with a drink in front of him.)

STANTON: *(enters, looking depressed)* I cannot believe I neva get 'em. Boss, I no can believe I neva get 'em!

DUKIE: I heard.

STANTON: First time! Sixteen years in this business and first time this ever happen to me.

DUKIE: You're forgetting the Rodney Okasako incident.

STANTON: That neva' count 'cause I wasn't driving the fork lift. But this. That Derek Pang is like one monstah Energizer Bunny. He just keep going and going and . . .

DUKIE: Boy, what had happen?

STANTON: Well, I was all set. I did all my homework. Had my plan all figured out. I knew what time Derek leaves, how long he take for come by the bridge, everything. Then I wen rig up the bridge over the Wailuku River with a thousand pounds of ammonium nitrate fuel oil. *(waits for* DUKIE *to be impressed)*

DUKIE: Okay. *(not impressed)*

STANTON: I got the fertilzer from Augie Moniz's Yard and Garden and I got the fuel oil from da Pump and Split Service Station. I get receipts. And I had em all perfect and the timing was on and then BOOM!

DUKIE: Aha . . .

STANTON: Yeah, the bridge wen blow like one manapua when you put em in the microwave too long. Ba-boom! Was perfect.

DUKIE: But it wasn't perfect, was it?

STANTON: I cannot believe it. Da fricken guy wen bounce. He wen bounce! Derek Pang's car goes flying off the bridge like one Hot Wheels racer, bradda Derek come flying out of the driver's seat, going, going, going ass over heels, and he land on top one banana tree. The thing wen bend back just like one cartoon. And then boingngng! Da tree wen bounce back and just fly Derek Pang back up on da hill. I no could believe. He landed like two feet away from me. Not one scratch on his body. Da guy is like Superman, Kikaida, Hulk Hogan, and Jackie Chan all rolled into one.

DUKIE: I'm disappointed in you.

STANTON: I know. I know.

DUKIE: What now?

STANTON: I get one Plan B.

DUKIE: Let's hear it.

STANTON: Okay. Dis is perfect. I wen work 'em all out. I was talking to Lawton Pacheco, and he told me . . .

DUKIE: Wait. You was talking to Puka Head Pacheco?

STANTON: Yeah. He give me good advice.

DUKIE: You taking advice from Puka Head Pacheco?

STANTON: He has a lot to say.

DUKIE: He has a puka in his head.

STANTON: I like to think he has an open mind. *(laughs at his own joke)*

DUKIE: *(not amused)* Go on.

STANTON: Okay. So Lawton told me Derek Pang is singing tonight in the district semi-finals for the Hawai'i Stars Karaoke Contest. So check this out. When he stay singing, he holding the mike, yeah? And all I gotta do is clip couple wires in the fuse box, reconnect one certain way and all that juice going go right back through the cable into his hand. Zzzzt! Derek Pang going fry like one malassada at the Hāwī Country Carnival.

DUKIE: Just get 'em right this time. I don't tolerate incompetence.

STANTON: Why? What you going do? Dock my pay? No can! You no pay me notting!

DUKIE: I keep you alive, boy.

STANTON: Yeah, and if I piss you off, who you going get for knock me off? You only get me. All the rest of your boys either in jail or in Queen's. It's like you running this business and everybody stay out on workman's comp.

DUKIE: I just about had it with you.

STANTON: Nah, boss. No worry. Sandra need da job done, I get 'em done.

DUKIE: Get it right.

STANTON: No worry, beef curry. I get satisfaction from a job well done. I betta hele 'cause I gotta stop by Yamashiro's Hardware and Bento before tonight.

DUKIE: Now you watch your step, boy.

STANTON: No worry. I da man. Stanton da manton. *(exits, fade to black)*

SCENE 8

(Sandra rushes across the stage with a fire hose coiled over one shoulder. She's holding a bag of cat chow. Her cell phone rings and she stops to answer it.)

SANDRA: This is Sandralene Leialoha Ferriera . . . . Oh! Howzit Mrs. Medeiros. How you? No, no more handi-van. No worry, I going take you to your doctor's appointment. But first, I gotta' feed the kitties at the Humane Society, put out one fire in Pana'ewa, and pick up one old ice box from the side of the road in Mountain View. No, I gotta' go put out the brush fire first. Big, you know. I cannot come pick you up first. Why, what you cooking? I'll be right there. *(exits)*

SCENE 9

(Outside the back of Jazzmin's. A beat-up door with peeling paint has a sign on it that says "Jazzmin's Karaoke and Washerette. Keep door closed so no bang when get wind." There is one window with very dirty panes. A fuse box is

next to the window. Muffled karaoke music can be heard.

STANTON enters, whistling and trying to act nonchalant. When he's sure he's alone, he pulls a large toolbox out from under his jacket. As he rummages through the box, he begins to talk to himself.)

STANTON: Okay. Okay. I get 'em now. All I gotta do is open up the fuse box, disconnect the blue wire and reconnect em on E 4 and that should do it. *(pause, listening)* Ho, dat Derek Pang. Some nice his voice. Yeah, too bad he ain't gonna make it to Hawai'i Stars. He really woulda blown Carole Kai's doors. Oh well, ten-thousand volts should do it. Too bad he not singing da Electric Slide. Ha! Here goes notting.

(STANTON connects two wires with a great flourish. There is a very loud hum like a surge of electricity and a loud zap as the music goes dead. There is a bright flash of light before everything goes dark.)

STANTON: Woo-hoo! I got 'em! . . . Wait! Oh no! Not again!

SCENE 10

(mayor's office, the next day)

SANDRA: *(enters)* Hoo! Howzit Mistah Mayah! Sorry I late. I wen stop by my Auntie's house on da way in 'cause she made me some pao dulce and was sooo good, hot and fresh from the . . . *(sees LESTER and DUKIE)* Dukie! What a surprise.

DUKIE: Aloha, Sandralene. *(kisses her cheek)*

LESTER: Sandra, I'd like you to meet my latest hire.

SANDRA: Your latest hire? Dukie, what is going on here? You guys yanking my leg or what? Where's da hidden camera? Dis gotta be one joke.

DUKIE: It's not a joke, Sandra.

LESTER: Dukie here is going to be my new Director of Security.

SANDRA: Director of Security?! What da hell you think this is? Da fricken Pentagon? Da position doesn't even exist!

LESTER: It does now.

SANDRA: Oh god.

LESTER: It's a very important position.

SANDRA: How important? Just as important as the position you created to keep Derek Pang quiet?

DUKIE: Actually, it's a little more important. Eight weeks vacation a year and a county car. I'm better at negotiating than Derek is.

SANDRA: So, what vitally important program did you cut to fund this job, Lester?

LESTER: I'm closing the Pana'ewa Zoo . . . and cutting your position to half time.

SANDRA: What?!

LESTER: That way, you can have more free time to pursue your other interests.

SANDRA: My other interests?! I have no other interests! All I've done my whole life is try to make this place a better place to live.

LESTER: Oh, come on now. Don't get all dramastical here. All you've done is organize some parties, answer a few phone calls, and chase me around because you knew I was the gravy train and you wanted a free ride.

SANDRA: I cannot believe I'm hearing this after all I did for you.

LESTER: It's not like I'm firing you. I'm just downsizing my staff a little to make room for a valuable new addition. And honey, you know you need some downsizing.

SANDRA: This is unreal. I feel like I'm on Ricki Lake during Freak Week. Lester, you wouldn't have gotten to be mayah if wasn't for me. I told you how to act. I told you what to say. I told you which babies to kiss and which babes not to get caught kissing. I drew up the county budget, Lester. Me. I did that. Why? 'Cause you no can do math. I wen write your campaign speeches. Me. I did that. Why? 'Cause if I didn't, you woulda just gone up to that microphone and lift up your hands like fricken Nixon and said "Vote for me. We probably related." And even though we haven't been in this office very long, every decision, every plan, every idea that came from the mayah's office that made a real difference for this town, it all came from me. All of it.

LESTER: Sounds like you need a break babe. You're stressing out. Good thing you'll be only working part-time now.

SANDRA: I cannot run this office part time. I cannot run this town part-time. And keeping your dumb ass out of trouble, that's a damn full time job right there.

LESTER: Think of it this way. You'll have more time to go to lunch.

SANDRA: My god. You really think that's all I do. You really have no idea, yeah? First of all, all I ever wanted to do with my life was make Hilo one better place to live, like it was back when my grandmadda's grandmadda was around.

Ever since I was a JPO in fourth grade, holding that stop
sign, blowing that whistle, I know I had the power to
stop the traffic, make people safe, help da keiki on da
path of life. Even when I was bringing in big time
wrestling to the Edith Kanaka'ole Stadium, I neva do em
fo make money. I was doing 'em fo give the youths in
Hilo something betta fo do than smoke pakalōlō and sell
ice.

DUKIE: Sandra, calm down. I understand you're upset right now.
(to LESTER) You should give her a couple of weeks off or
something.

LESTER: I cannot. My State of the County Address is scheduled
for next week, and she neva tell me what I going say yet.

SANDRA: And you, Dukie! What the hell is happening here? You
hate Lester. You said he had less brains than a flat
mongoose on the Māmalahoa Highway.

DUKIE: I changed my mind.

SANDRA: You selling out.

DUKIE: Sandra, I cannot live the thug life forever. I gotta step
aside for the new class to rise up in the ranks . . . like that
one kid, Tupac Shakur Medeiros. He's going to be a real
player someday. Anyways, my back is sore, my knees all
buss and my eyesight ain't what it used to be. Time for
me to hang up my brass knuckles and go where all the
old syndicate guys go to retire.

SANDRA: Florida?

DUKIE: Politics. You not thinking straight about this, cousin. Me
in this job can only help you. I get power. I get drag. I
can be close and protect you when you need me.

SANDRA: I'll never ask for your help again. I don't need your help.

DUKIE: Oh, you need my help, all right. You needed my help even to win that silly beauty pageant congeniality runner-up thing.

SANDRA: If you had any drag at all, I would have won da crown.

DUKIE: You need me, Sandralene. You no mo anybody else now. You need me.

(DUKIE and SANDRA glare at each other)

LESTER: *(trying to break up the tension)* Well, now. How about we all three go to lunch somewhere together. Make some plans. Plan some stuff. Tina Tunta's Pastele Wagon is just down the street today.

SANDRA: You guys go. I don't feel like eating. But make sure you have a little extra, for me.

(DUKIE and LESTER exit. Fade to black)

SCENE 11

(Behind Jazzmin's)

STANTON: *(enters, tool box in hand, looking frustrated and dejected)* Suckin' fricken' unreal Derek Pang. Why he no just die already? Ten-thousand volts and all he get is one small-kine afro. I no can believe! Bradda like dat coyote-guy on the Road Runner cartoon. Fall over one cliff, get electrocuted, anykind, and he still walking around. *(while speaking, puts down the tool box, opens it and rummages around.)* But third time gotta be da charmer. Okay, I get my blueprints of Jazzmin's, my remote control race car control thing, WHICH I have cleverly re-wired to send radio signals to the ceiling fan over Derek Pang's favorite table . . . and I get—*(cell phone rings)* Shoot. Hello? Dis

Stanton. Who dis? Lawton, das you? Lawton, das you? Lawton, das you? Puka Head, das you eh? Eh, I busy, Puka. I no can talk right now. What you like? What I doing? I trying fo' rig up da ceiling fan at Jazzmin's so the ting just go off like one airplane propeller. No, I wen rig dis radio control thing. Nah, going work. Going work. I seen how for do 'em on one show on cable. *Martha Stewart's Living.* Das' right. When Derek Pang sit under that thing, I just going let 'em go and going spin supa' fast, fly off the ceiling, and aloha 'oe. It slices, it dices, it minces, grates, and chops. Gross, yeah? Yeah, going work. Going work! Eh, no call me stupid. No call me stupid. Eh, Puks, I not da one wid da puka in my head so if I was you I wouldn't talk. I gotta go already. You throwing me off. Yeah, I pick you up after. We can go down Pana'ewa dump, go shoot rat. 'Kay. Laters. *(puts away phone)* Okay, here it goes. Open the antenna, turn 'em on. Nothing. Shoot! Batteries! *(goes through a big production to find batteries and put them into the remote control)* Okay. Now, turn 'em on, twist the switch and we're off!

> *(Sound of a propeller or rotor slowly turning, getting faster and faster. It starts to sound like a helicopter.)*

Woo-hoo! Derek, I get you now!

> *(Along with the propeller sound, another sound appears—the sound of boards creaking, straining and ultimately breaking)*

(looks up) Ay ke Jesus! No ways! NO! Not da roof! OH NO!

> *(fade to black)*

SCENE 12

(Inside Jazzmin's, the next day)

(STANTON walks in, extremely dejected and depressed. His head hangs low, feet shuffling. He sighs greatly and shakes his head. He walks to the table where DUKIE sits waiting with a drink in front of him.)

STANTON: Aaaahhhhh . . .

DUKIE: Sit the hell down. I gotta say, you suck as a hit-man, but you even worse as an interior decorator.

STANTON: Yeah. I don't know what happened.

DUKIE: I'll tell you what happened. You screwed up again. You made the fan fly through the roof with half of Jazzmin's ceiling still attached, and you left me with one big repair bill.

STANTON: Boss, I sorry. I fix da roof for you. I real good at construction, so long as I no do too much with electronics.

DUKIE: Forget it. I want you gone.

STANTON: But wait. Boss, I figured it out. I was just getting too fancy with Derek. I gotta just get back to the basics. Stick to my fundamentals. I was thinking all I gotta do is one good old-fashioned execution-style shooting and that would be it.

DUKIE: You off da job, and you out of here.

STANTON: What you mean "out of here"?

DUKIE: I not carrying you no more, boy. You out of this town. You out of Hilo.

STANTON: But dis is my home! Hilo is my place. Sandra is here.

DUKIE: Get out. Go live Honolulu or something.

STANTON: *(gasps)* Honolulu! Not Honolulu! Dukie, listen. I know I can get this hit right. I just need one more chance at Derek Pang.

DUKIE: You keep your hands off Derek Pang. Don't you go near him. You understand? The hit is off.

STANTON: But Sandra needs me to do it.

DUKIE: Sandra needs a good hobby and a good slap. And I need you out of here.

STANTON: Boss . . .

DUKIE: I'm going out to lunch with the mayor. When I come back, I want you packed up and gone. You got it?

STANTON: But Boss, what you going do without me? I your right hand man.

DUKIE: I have a new ally now, a Mister Derek Pang. And I have a new stooge, too, Mayor Lester Perez . . . and he's going to buy me lunch.

(*DUKIE exits, STANTON slumps at the table.*)

Daryl Bonilla, BullDog, Stu Hirayama, Ly Atsumi.

ACT II

SCENE 1

(Jazzmin's Karaoke Bar and Washerette.
STANTON sits alone.)

SANDRA: *(enters, noticeably depressed)* Hey, Stanton. How you? Long time no spock, yeah?

STANTON: Hey.

SANDRA: Hoo! Whassa matta' wich you? You look like you ate one of Tina Tunta's Pasteles.

STANTON: *(manages a smile)* Nah, dat shit'll kill you.

SANDRA: The murder-for-hire business not going well?

STANTON: Well, it's not really murder for hire. I never got paid. I just got like other stuff. It's more like murder for trade.

SANDRA: Oh.

STANTON: I'm sorry, Sandra. You know, I'm just kinda sitting here feeling all junk and stuff. I kind of embarrassed you seeing me like this.

SANDRA: Don't be silly. We old friends, right? To tell you da truth, I feeling kinda junkalunka too.

STANTON: You? I thought you never have a bad day.

SANDRA: I've had planny hard times in my life.

STANTON: I know that. Das' not what I mean. It's just—no matter what, you always seem like you come up on top . . . like da way da fat rises to the top of the beef curry when you put 'em in the ice box. Das' you. *(pauses, realizes what he has just said)* OH! God, das not how I meant 'em fo come out. I mean, I think of you as da rainbow that follows the Hilo rain.

SANDRA: Das' really nice. I didn't know you was one poet.

STANTON: Oh yeah! I wrote planny stuffs when I was, uh, a guest of the State Public Safety department.

SANDRA: Really?!

STANTON: Poems, stories, songs, anykind.

SANDRA: I would love to read some of your stuff.

STANTON: Oh, kinda hard 'cause I neva really have paper, yeah, in jail . . . so I mostly just wrote my poems on da walls.

SANDRA: Oh.

STANTON: Sorry. *(beat)* Oh wait! I wen tattoo couple poems on my body wit one piece sharp wire and India ink. I get one nice one on my thigh. Try let me find 'em.

SANDRA: Uh, that's okay, Stanton.

STANTON: Okay. Maybe some odda time den. *(pause)* So what's making you so bum out?

SANDRA: Aaahhh . . . It's just, it's just so hard when you give somebody all you have, you know? Everything you have. Your heart, your brain, your reputation. You do all the work, they take all the glory, and you're left with notting except more messes to clean up.

STANTON: And one butter knife.

SANDRA: What?

STANTON: Nothing. Long story. Sorry.

SANDRA: I get dreams, you know. Big dreams. But sometimes, all the stuff getting in my way just seems big like Mauna Loa.

STANTON: But people climb Mauna Loa all the time.

SANDRA: Look at you. You one sweetie, I tell you. You stay all bum out yourself, but you trying so hard for cheer me up. I should be trying to make *you* feel better.

STANTON: Jus' being in your presence makes me feel better. You like one dose Pepto Bismol after you eat too much pickled mango. You make things all right.

SANDRA: Check you out, Mister Rico Suave. I neva know you had such a way wid words.

STANTON: Ah, I spent planny time in da prison library.

SANDRA: So what's bodderating you anyways?

STANTON: Ah, same old stuff as everybody else. Bad week at the office. Da boss is really on my back. Overworked and underpaid. You know how it goes.

SANDRA: You got dat right.

STANTON: You know, you and me get planny stuff in common.

SANDRA: Like what?

STANTON: Like we both work for guys dat no appreciate us.

SANDRA: Yeah.

STANTON: And we both no eat Puerto Rican food.

SANDRA: Not from Tina Tunta's I don't.

STANTON: And we both part Albanian.

SANDRA: No kidding? You get Albanian blood too? You no look Albanian.

STANTON: Oh sure. My grandmother was from Albany.

SANDRA: Oh.

STANTON: And we both want to be more than we are right now. I get big dreams too, you know.

SANDRA: Oh yeah? Tell me your dreams.

STANTON: Ah, it sounds silly. But ever since I was one small kid, I wanted to drive around those sampans in Hilo town. Show everybody all da sights. Act all Mister Aloha and stuff.

SANDRA: *(laughing)* For real?

STANTON: Yeah, I know as kinda lōlō, but I wanted for see da world but I neva really wanted to leave dis town. So I figure if I drive around in one sampan, da world would come to visit me. I would meet all kind people and they would be all happy 'cause they was in Hawai'i on their dream vacation in paradise. And I wouldn't bullshit them with tourist crap stories. I would tell them all da kind stories my tutu used to tell me . . . the real stuff about Hawai'i, you know? And I would know how to treat all the stars and dignitaries just the way they like to be treated. And people from around da world would write me letters and send me pictures of their kids Christmastime. *(beat)* Ah, no even get sampans anymore. I guess I missed my chance.

SANDRA: You unreal, Stanton. I neva know you was so dakine.

STANTON: Nah.

SANDRA: For real. Stan, you da man. Stanton, you *are* da manton.

STANTON: Ah, tanks, eh. From you, das da most beautiful thing I ever heard.

SANDRA: *You* should be da mayah's Director of Protocol. You would be perfect for da job.

STANTON: Eh, dat would be so unreal.

SANDRA: You could greet visiting dignitaries and show them around town . . .

STANTON: Yeah! Maybe even start up the sampans again.

SANDRA: And you could be the most charming security guard at the big functions.

STANTON: I'd knock 'em dead—so to speak. Oh Sandra, would be so perfeck, except for one thing.

SANDRA: What's that?

STANTON: Would be perfeck if you was my babes.

SANDRA: Ay, Stanton!

STANTON: I know. I sorry. I just cannot hold back how I feel already. I so ono for you. I even wrote a song about it.

SANDRA: You neva!

STANTON: I did.

SANDRA: Go sing 'em.

STANTON: Nah.

SANDRA: Go!

STANTON: I no can.

SANDRA: I like hear 'em.

STANTON: Shame!

SANDRA: If you sing 'em, I'll make you my County Director of Protocol when I'm mayah.

STANTON: I'd rather be your man.

SANDRA: My manton.

STANTON: *(rushes to karaoke machine and grabs the mike)* Hit it!

My life is so junk without you
Like large saimin, no mo' shoyu
Like musubi without ume,
I feel so empty when you no stay

Wen grind out at my friend's luau
Went Tutu's house, ate bacalhau
I stay so full, feel like I going buss
But my heart is hungry without us

My kitchen's full of food, baby (baby)
But I still yet ono for you

I made six trips through the buffet
The waiter told me for go away
But no plate lunch and no beef stew
Can fill me up the way you do

I wen eat lunch Sam Choy's baby (baby)
But I still yet ono for you

I crave your kisses on my lips
Like Frito Lay brand taro chips
You soft and sweet like haupia
My mouth all water when I see ya

Get all the food I like baby (baby)
But I still yet ono for you

But I would give up all my grinds
If you would say you would be mines
Would even give up pinakbet
If you told me get chance yet

If you was mine, it would be so neat
Then both us two could go out fo eat
I wouldn't have to eat all alone
We'd get take out and go grind at home

Get all the food I like baby (baby)
But I still yet ono for you

SCENE 2

(Jazzmin's)

DUKIE: *(enters holding a take-out plate lunch container in his hand)* Stanton! I thought I told you to get out of town!

SANDRA: You leave him alone, Dukie.

DUKIE: Stay out of this, Sandralene. Dis is between me and him.

STANTON: It's okay, Sandra.

DUKIE: You, shut up. And you. *(looks at SANDRA)* Isn't there something else you'd rather be doing, like feeding your face at Santiago's Chinese Kitchen or something.

STANTON: Hey! Don't talk to her that way!

DUKIE: I'll talk to my cousin any way I want. I've been hauling her ass out of trouble ever since we was six years old and Merwin Caldites wanted to give her lickens behind the school cafeteria because she ate his sister Merwina's lunch. I practically own her.

STANTON: Nobody own nobody.

DUKIE: I OWN YOU. I want you out of here NOW.

SANDRA: Oh yeah. What you going do, Dukie? You no mo nobody left fo do all your dirty work. No mo nobody left who would stand behind you and your threats. And you not going do nothing yourself. You da perfect county employee—all show and no go.

DUKIE: I'll call the police.

STANTON: Ha! The police! I thought you was allergic to cops.

DUKIE: I'll tell them everything.

SANDRA: Bullshet. Like they'd even listen to one thug like you.

STANTON: You would only incriminate yourself.

DUKIE: You're forgetting. I'm the County Director of Security. I oversee all the workings of the police department *and* the prosecutor's office.

SANDRA: What?!

DUKIE: I'm a regular Janet Reno.

STANTON: Yeah, but even she's betta looking.

DUKIE: So you see, you have two choices, boy. Get out of town now, or I'll have you back in Kulani Correctional by tomorrow morning, sharing a cell with Mad Dog Morikawa. And this time, there won't be no parole. Maybe Lester and I can discuss legislation to enact the death penalty in Hilo for mass murderers.

SANDRA: Knock it off, Dukie. Stanton is the best man you eva' had. You should be putting him on your county payroll instead of making these threats.

DUKIE: No threats. Only a promise. I promise, if you don't leave Hilo right now, I will get you and take away everything you have.

STANTON: *(pulls butter knife out of pocket and looks at it sadly. To SANDRA)* I better go, Sandra. At least for a while.

SANDRA: Where you going go, baby?

STANTON: I don't know. I guess . . . Honolulu.

SANDRA: *(absolutely shocked)* Not Honolulu!

STANTON: I going be okay. I going miss Hilo, though. I going miss the rain and the rainbows and the smell of Hilo Harbor in the afternoon when the akule is running. All dat stuff. But mostly, I going miss you.

SANDRA: I'll come with you.

STANTON: *(softly)* What?

SANDRA: I no mo' notting left here anyways. Except my Mother-them, but she would love to come up visit me in Honolulu, go shopping Sam's Club, buy the 64-pack toilet paper. Besides, she driving me crazy with her Senior Citizens Jiu Jitsu Ultimate Fighting.

STANTON: You would really move Honolulu with me?

SANDRA: We could get one nice house together in Kalihi.

STANTON: *Upper* Kalihi.

SANDRA: And I could find one good-paying office job.

STANTON: Maybe work for OHA or Bishop Estate.

SANDRA: A job where everybody in the office get aloha and support each other and work like one team.

STANTON: Oh. *Not* OHA or Bishop Estate.

SANDRA: Maybe go back to promoting women's wrestling on the side.

STANTON: I'll take good care of you, Sandra. I'll take you to the best plate lunch places and get you membership cards at Sam's Club and Costco and all those stores. I'll take you to Aloha Stadium Swap Meet every Saturday and Sunday and drive you to Puamana Crabbe's factory outlet so you can buy your muumuus direct, at cost. Going be so good, Sandra. we go leave tonight.

SANDRA: I meet you Aloha Airlines counter. I get my executive club card, so we can be first on the plane. Last flight to Honolulu.

STANTON: Last flight to Honolulu.

SANDRA: Dis so romantic! Jess like da afternoon movies on Lifetime Television for Women. I betta go before I start crying like one baby.

DUKIE: Just go already. You guys making me sick.

SANDRA: *(starts to leave, and then turns to DUKIE)* You know, you act like I owe you something and I don't owe you nothing. All those times I helped you wid your problems when we was kids, I listened to you. I told you you was all bad. I wen build up your confidence when you was all futless. We cousins, and look at how you act. I just get one more thing to tell you. Remember the time was junior prom and you was all in love with Claudette Minervis and you wen ask her out and you thought she would tell you yeah cuz you was the bull of the school but she just when laugh in your face and said you was ugly. Den she went prom with dat buss-up-teeth-guy Irwin Pupuka. And you was all nuts and depressed and you came to me and asked me if you was ugly—more ugly dan Irwin Pupuka and I told you no. You remember?

DUKIE: Yeah.

SANDRA: I lied. *(exits)*

DUKIE: Get out of here, Stanton.

STANTON: I'm going. I'm going. Eh, you no look so good, boss.

DUKIE: I'm fine. Now get out.

STANTON: I will. But for real. Your face get one funny color . . . kinda like the color of squid lū'au.

DUKIE: My stomach hurts a little.

STANTON: What you wen eat for lunch?

DUKIE: Pasteles.

STANTON: Not from Tina Tunta's! Boss, I told you, she serving surplus rations she found in one abandoned World War Two bunker in Hakalau.

DUKIE: Aaaah ! *(gets up and holds his hand to his mouth and rushes offstage)*

STANTON: *(to himself)* Wid all da good plate lunches in this town, I don't know why he insists on eating that pilau pasteles. Not when get so much good stuff . . . like ox-tail soup, spam musubi, kal bi ribs, three-choice Korean plate, wor won ton, 'opihi saimin . . .

DUKIE: *(enters, looking ill)* Aaah.

STANTON: You okay, boss?

DUKIE: Yeah. Now get out of here. I don't want to see you . . . *(stops cold, puts one hand to his mouth and one to his stomach, eyes suddenly wide open)* 'Scuse me. *(runs offstage)*

STANTON: Ooo, round two. Okay, where I was? Oh yeah. 'Opihi saimin, fried rice, fried rice with egg, loco moco with egg, stew and rice with egg, Portuguese sausage with egg, omelet with egg . . .

(DUKIE reappears, looking worse.)

Boss! Here, sit down little while. I'll get you some water. What is this, leftovers from lunch? *(opens styrofoam container)* Whoa! Dat is fricken hauna!

(DUKIE again runs offstage, holding his hand to his mouth)

Man! I neva smell something that stink since I had to dig up Colton Carvalho and bury him in one safer place.

(DUKIE enters)

Man, you look like how my mada wen look when she took up on one trip on SeaFlight. You rememba' that? SeaFlight? That stupid hydrofoil thing was supposed to be like one inter-island ferry thing but people said was whacking whales.

DUKIE: Mmmmm . . . . *(nods weakly)*

STANTON: So what? Stay coming out one end or the other.

DUKIE: *(answers with great difficulty)* Both.

STANTON: Boss, I know you like me leave, but you gotta let me take care of you. Just until you feel better. Then I'll go Honolulu. I promise.

DUKIE: Get the hell away from me.

STANTON: Boss, you coming out like 'Akaka Falls on both ends. You need me.

DUKIE: I don't need your . . . *(pause, struggling, very ill)* help!

(DUKIE collapses to the floor. STANTON rushes to him, kneels, checks for a pulse, and listens for breathing.)

STANTON: You okay, boss. You going be okay. I going take you hospital. No worry. I just going take you to the car.

(STANTON keeps talking to the unconscious DUKIE, trying to reassure him. STANTON tries to lift him, but he is too heavy. STANTON tries numerous times to pick him up, lifting different parts of his body, to no avail. STANTON grabs his legs and tries to drag him out, but can only move him a few feet, even with great effort. STANTON finally manages to move him by flopping him over and rolling him, with much strain and effort, flopping across the stage.)

Man, I've moved some bodies in my life, but this is
ridicuous.

(Both exit the stage.)

SCENE 3

(mayor's office)

SANDRA: *(enters, obviously dejected. She is carrying an empty box.
The office is quiet as she goes about cleaning off her desk,
putting things in the box. She looks at each item sadly. After
a while, she starts to notice how quiet everything is.)* Mistah
Mayah? Where you stay? Mistah Mayah? Wow, dat's
weird. He's always here when I get in . . . 'cause every day
he gotta wait for me tell him what to do before he go out
and do 'em. *(to herself)* Hoo, I gonna miss dis place. I had
some good times in this office. The powerful woman
running the government behind the scenes—that's me.
One regular Vicky Cayetano. I'll be back, though. I don't
know how, I don't know when. But just like onions on a
bad plate lunch, I'll be back, stronger than ever.

STANTON: *(bursts in)* Sandra! Sandra, you gotta come quick!

SANDRA: Stanton, for crying out loud. What's wrong?

STANTON: Your cousin Dukie. He's sick.

SANDRA: What?! What happened?!

STANTON: He collapsed at Jazzmin's. Just ba-doom, huli on the
floor like one sack rotten potatoes.

SANDRA: Oh no!

STANTON: But wait! Get more! I wen drive him emergency room and I get there, fly open the doors, drag him inside, and you not going believe who was there . . . Derek Pang!

SANDRA: What?!

STANTON: All green. Full palu-action. The two of them. Its bad, Sandra.

SANDRA: Oh, man. I better get down there.

STANTON: C'mon. I'll drive you. I gotta warn you but, it don't look good.

SANDRA: Ay ke Jesus. How terrible! What if they die!

STANTON: Yeah, but even worse—what if they live.

> (SANDRA and STANTON exchange a knowing
> look. They start to leave. LESTER enters and
> they almost bump into each other.)

LESTER: Where do you think you're going?

SANDRA: Lester! My cousin Dukie stay emergency room!

LESTER: So?

SANDRA: He's sick! And Derek Pang, too! I bet you was those pilau pasteles.

LESTER: That's redickalous. I ate the same thing for lunch, and look at me. I'm the picture of health.

STANTON: That ain't a pretty picture.

SANDRA: You better come hospital with us.

STANTON: Maybe they running a special . . . pump two stomachs and the third one is free!

LESTER: Have you finished my State of the County Address yet?

SANDRA: What?!

LESTER: You're not going anywhere until you finish my State of the County Address. My speech is scheduled for this afternoon, and I hear the cable public access channel is going to carry it. This is my big chance to get on TV.

SANDRA: What, Jerry Springer neva' return your calls? Listen, Lester, I telling you, you gotta' go doctor *now*. But if you no like listen to me, after all the good advice I gave you, fine. Suffer. No come crying to me when you dead.

   (SANDRA and STANTON exit.)

LESTER: Ha! Pilau pasteles. Right. Look at me. I'm fine.

   (All of a sudden, LESTER collapses in a heap on the floor like a puppet whose strings have been cut. Lights fade. There is the sound of an EKG machine. The heartbeat continues for several seconds before the infamous steady tone of a "flat-line" is heard.)

SCENE 4

   (funeral parlor)

SANDRA: *(stands alone, weeping over a closed coffin. She is bawling most dramatically. After a long period of crying, she looks around her to make sure she is alone. Satisfied that she is, she stops crying immediately, straightens up, and gives the coffin a hard whack with her hand.)* Ganfannit you bastard! What the hell were you thinking? Oh, I so mad. Look the mess you left behind. If you wasn't dead already, I would fricken kill you for this! *(starts crying loudly again.)*

   (STANTON enters. He walks over to SANDRA and puts his arm around her to console her.)

Oh God, I no can believe he is gone, Stanton. I no can believe.

STANTON: I know. I know.

SANDRA: I mean, he was here, all mouth and big talking, and then he just poof, gone away so fast. Just like Chris Hemmeter.

STANTON: Yeah. Death is funny that way, you know? It's so . . . fatal, yeah?

SANDRA: Yeah. I mean, had so much times I wanted fo kill him, but I neva like him *die*, you know?

STANTON: Yeah, me too.

SANDRA: He used my brains for get ahead. He used my heart against me. He used my body for, ah, who the hell knows. I was asleep half the time, he was so junk.

STANTON: *(pulls away)* What?! What you saying?! You and Dukie was da-kining?!

SANDRA: Dukie?! Jesus, no! Dukie and me is cousins. I mean, Dukie and me was cousins. I was talking about Lester.

STANTON: Wait. That's Dukie in there.

SANDRA: Das' Lester.

STANTON: No, wait. I think that's Dukie.

SANDRA: Get one "Perez for Mayor" bumper sticker on this side. Gotta be Lester.

STANTON: Ay, you sure?

SANDRA: You gotta check.

STANTON: I no like check.

SANDRA: You gotta check.

STANTON: How I going check?

SANDRA: Look.

STANTON: I no like look.

SANDRA: We gotta find out. We gotta look.

STANTON: Sandra, there's a reason why they made 'um one closed coffin service.

SANDRA: Why?

STANTON: Stink.

SANDRA: No. No can be stink. The undertaker when embalm him and stuff.

STANTON: Maybe it's because he look extra ugly.

SANDRA: They both was extra ugly when they was alive. No make difference.

STANTON: You know, maybe you shouldn't look one last time. This could be too dramastical for you.

SANDRA: I can handle it. Believe me, I seen worse things than Lester dead . . . like Lester naked *(shudders)*. Please, Stanton, look inside for me. I like know who it is so I know how much money fo put inside the envelope.

STANTON: Why?

SANDRA: If it's Lester, I going put less. Dat fricka borrowed twenty bucks from me da day he died *(starts crying)* and now I neva going get 'em back!

STANTON: Don't cry, Sandralene. Don't cry. Look, I'll check for you. It's okay. *(summons up his courage and with great care and hesitation, takes a deep breath and opens up the coffin. He looks in and lets out a loud scream, slamming the coffin shut.)*

SANDRA: What! What! Who is it?!

STANTON: *(panting and heaving, very shaken up)* I don't know.

SANDRA: You don't know?!

STANTON: Wrong side. All I saw was feet. And let me tell you, those feet freaked me the hell out. *(pause to catch his breath)* Okay. I'll try the other side.

SANDRA: Go try the other side.

> *(STANTON repeats procedure of opening the coffin very carefully. He looks in and screams, but stops cold mid-scream.)*

SANDRA: What! Who is it?!

STANTON: I don't know.

SANDRA: Oh my god, is it that bad you cannot even tell?

STANTON: No. I mean, I don't know this guy. I no even reckanotice his face. As one old Japanese dude.

SANDRA: One old Japanese dude?!

STANTON: Yeah. I neva seen dis bugga before in my life. Nice aloha shirt, though. I wonder where he got it from. I should check the tag. *(reaches into the coffin)*

SANDRA: You mean das not Dukie or Lester?

STANTON: We at the wrong funeral.

SANDRA: I was wondering why Lester's funeral would be held at one Hongwanji.

STANTON: Come. We go.

SANDRA: 'Kay. Wait, try wait. *(speaking to coffin)* Trust me, you don't want to go into the hereafter with this thing stuck on top. *(rips off bumper sticker)* Hey, I'm sorry for all that stuff I was saying before. I neva mean you. I sure you was one very nice old Japanese dude. The kind of man who never took advantage of anybody or told them that you would leave your wife for them and make them wait fifteen years for notting while you wife getting more rich and more fat, all the while that person is doing all your work for you and you getting all the praise and the bucks and you just cruising while they stay busting ass and . . .

STANTON: Sandra, it's okay. It's okay. Let it go. As' all pau already.

SANDRA: Yeah, you're right. I'm just still so mad.

STANTON: If there's one thing I've learned in my career, it's that dead guys no feel sorry. Maybe they sorry right before they die, be once they dead, they kinda don't give a rip.

SANDRA: But see, that's what pisses me off the most about Lester. He never gave a rip about anyone, ever. I know how he treated me was wrong, but I have to admit I let him get away with it. I had the choice to leave, but I stayed. But what really boils my onions is that he neva give a rip about the people of this town. Here he was, the first mayor of Hilo, and he never once asked himself, "How am I going to make a difference in this town?" "How am I going to make life better for these people?" Not once! I get so sick of these fricken politicians acting like they going save the world during campaign time and then once they get in office, spending all their energy working on ways to stay in office and get free golf clubs and free trips to Asia and secure a future serving as a do-nothing board member of a wealthy trust. These people supposed to be public servants, not *have* public servants!

STANTON: Ho, Sandralene, kūʻē!

SANDRA: I know. It's just, Lester always accused me of only caring about power muumuus and greeting dignitaries and ordering lunch, but he was the one acting like a queen in a castle while I was Cinderella wiping up all the messes.

STANTON: But in the end, Cinderella got to go to the ball.

SANDRA: *(smiling a little)* Yeah.

STANTON: And when she got there, I bet she wen dance her ass off.

SANDRA: She wen blow *everybody's* doors.

STANTON: Come. We go eat. Ten-thirty already. Time for lunch.

SANDRA: I don't know if I feel like eating.

STANTON: There's a new Filipino food place just around the corner. I heard the pinakbet is excellent.

SANDRA: Oh, alright. Maybe just a mini-plate.

(*SANDRA and STANTON exit, arm in arm.*)

SCENE 5

(*on the steps of the county building*)

STANTON: Ladies and gentlemen, and all my friends from Brother Rocky Auwai's School of Hair Design, it is my pleasure to introduce Hilo County acting Mayor, Sandralene Leialoha Ferreira.

SANDRA: Thanks, yeah, everybody. I gotta tell you, just couple weeks ago, if somebody would have told me was going be me instead of Lester Perez giving this State of the County Address, I woulda' told 'em "crazy!" . . . and, I would have written a better speech. Hilo has suffered a loss with the death of Mayor Lester Perez, a good and decent man who served as . . .

(*STANTON coughs and clears his throat.*)

A good man who...

(*STANTON coughs and interrupts again.*)

A guy who you voted in as Hilo's first mayor.

STANTON: No blame me. I voted for Bu.

SANDRA: Let me assure you, the county prosecutor is pressing charges against Tina Tunta for three counts of negligent homicide for the horrible botulism incident. The responsible party will not go unpunished.

STANTON: I think you mean "unrewarded."

SANDRA: We just all so thankful that on the day of the poisonings, Tina Tunta only sold those three pastele lunches, because ordinarily she would sell couple hundred plates in a day.

STANTON: Uncanny, isn't it?

SANDRA: On behalf of the County of Hilo, I would like to thank you for all the generous outpouring of aloha during this difficult time. Why, just this week, our office received how many sympathy cards, Stanton?

STANTON: One.

SANDRA: Which brings the total number of sympathy cards to…

STANTON: Two.

SANDRA: Chee, I gotta' tell you, that's kinda' sad. But that's okay. That's okay, 'cause together we going work as a community to *imua*, move forward into the new millennium.

STANTON: That's millenimum. No. Wait. Sorry. You had 'em right.

SANDRA: We have restored the county funding to the Humane Society Healthy Puppy–Healthy Kitty program. We have re-established the Senior Citizens Handi-Van service, and we have re-built the Wailuku River Bridge, which was totaled by a mysterious and completely anonymous bombing just last month.

STANTON: Das' right. Was anonymous. Nobody know who.

SANDRA: But the most important question is, who going take over permanently in the mayor's office?

STANTON: Actually, Sandra, I think so I get the answer for that one. *(takes over the mike and holds up a large book)* I spent the whole day looking for this bugga' here. Fricken bradda Lester Perez was using his county books on protocol and procedure for hold back the door in the county building men's room so the thing no bang when get wind. But I wen locate 'em. *(starts looking through the pages)* Okay, according to the Hilo County Revised Administrative Statutes Rules and Regulations Section 36-24-36C, upon the pasteles botulism death of the elected mayor, oh, wait. Section C is for car accidents and cannibalism. Section A is for Axecution. Here it is, Section B for death by baseball bat, billy goat, and botulism . . . okay, the job goes automatically to . . . his administrative assistant. Sandra, that's you! You not acting Mayor, you for real!

SANDRA: What? No gotta make election or something first?

STANTON: No need election. You in!

SANDRA: Ay my god! I thought I was going to have to make election first. What I going do with all my uku-thousand bumper stickers I when make?

STANTON: No worry. Me and Lawton Pacheco take 'em off your hands. Take 'em Pana'ewa dump, go trap rat. Maybe can plug up the puka in Puka Head's head with the extras.

SANDRA: So what. You like be my new County Director of Protocol?

STANTON: *(wipes away a tear)* Shoot.

SANDRA: Stanton, you are the da manton!

STANTON: I may be the manton, but Sandra, you da mayah!

Lee Cataluna's first play, *Da Mayah* was a box office hit when it premiered at Kumu Kahua Theatre in 1998. Subsequent productions at Kumu Kahua, the Maui Community Theater, and the University of Hawai'i at Hilo played to packed houses. Her play *Aloha Friday* won the Hawai'i award of the Kumu Kahua/UH Mānoa play writing contest. Other productions include *Ulua: The Musical* and *Super Secret Squad* at Kumu Kahua Theatre; *You Somebody* at Diamond Head Theatre; and *Musubi Man*, an adaptation of the book by Sandi Takayama, at Honolulu Theatre for Youth. Lee is a columnist for *The Honolulu Advertiser.*

Ka Wai Ola
the living water

by Victoria Nalani Kneubuhl

Ka Wai Ola:
Learning and Teaching
J. Wat

Victoria Kneubuhl recalls that in 1997, Peter Brosius, then the artistic director of Honolulu Theatre for Youth was interested in the work of the Reppuns, a family of activist taro farmers. Brosius approached her about writing a play that might deal with some of the issues surrounding their struggles. The play that Kneubuhl wrote for the HTY commission turned out to be about the issues of water rights and power, and related ecological issues, not specifically about the Reppuns or about the water struggles that were in the courts and the news at the time. "The play didn't end up being specifically about Waiahole-Waikane. I didn't want it to be a history of that valley because then it gets too restrictive," Kneubuhl says.

She did, though, read extensively to research the material for the play. She still has a file which includes technical articles on the Waiahole Ditch; philosophical articles, including Bachelot's "Imagination and Water;" many news articles about the case; and legal briefs, including the complete brief prepared by the Sierra Club Legal Defense Fund and the Native Hawaiian Legal Corporation for presentation to the Commission on Water Resource Management. In addition to her reading, she also attended some of the hearings about the case.

Kneubuhl says that there is usually an educational component to her plays and that she likes to do a lot of research for them. "More so in this play [*Ka Wai Ola*] than in my other children's plays because to me it's such a big issue and it was the first time I was writing a play that was about the environment and I really love the physical setting of our island. So I felt that it was really important. And boy did I learn a lot about water. I didn't know a lot of that stuff, you know, about whoever has the water rights, they've got all the money. People, I think, in general don't realize that, because without water you cannot do anything."

Although most of her plays have been written for adult audiences, several of them (including *Tofa Samoa* and *Paniolo Spurs*, also written for HTY) have been directed at younger audiences. *Ka Wai Ola* was written for fourth, fifth and sixth graders which Kneubuhl says is her "favorite age to write for because they're old enough to reason but young enough so their imaginations haven't been spoiled." Kneubuhl says that the difference between writing for a young audience and writing for adults is that "when you write for an audience like that [children] you really have to be on your toes, because grownups will go along with you for awhile to see what's going to happen. But kids, they cut you no slack. It has to be, every minute, the best you can write."

Being Hawaiian affects some of her works more than others, says Kneubuhl. For some of her plays, like *Story of Susannah*, being Hawaiian does not play a large role in the writing. But for other works, like *Ka Wai Ola*, being Hawaiian makes a difference. "Of course, if you're writing about this place that we're living in and you're someone like me who's part Hawaiian, then it's going to be a big factor. And when it's about an issue like that [water rights], it becomes an even bigger factor."

Kneubuhl notes that there was a lot of community support for *Ka Wai Ola*. "It's really nice that that community really helped that project. [*Kumu Hula*] Vicky Takamine came in at a certain point to help Kati [Kuroda, the director]. [*Kupuna* and artist] Calvin Hoe and the Reppuns were very supportive of the project. And the amazing thing is I got all these letters from teachers that were really supportive. And the play is a little political so I wasn't sure how teachers would react. And I think out of maybe forty letters there's only one of them that was irritated by the play. Most of the letters were grateful that there was a play about a contemporary issue that they could talk about with the kids." Kneubuhl also thinks that children find challenging theater engaging. "I think there's a lot of room for that kind of theater for children, that's about current issues; and I wish theaters would want to do more of it, because, if it's done in a really good way, kids like it. They like good, quality theatre about real issues, imagine that."

Finally, Kneubuhl comments on her play and the profound wellspring of culture that it draws from. "I really like that little play, *Ka Wai Ola*. One of the things I really liked was that I could put that stuff about *Kane* and the water. All that rich symbolism that is there in Hawaiian *mo'olelo*. It's amazing isn't it, *akamai, ka poe kahiko*."

Cynthia See, Walter Eccles, Kyle Kakuno.

KA WAI OLA:
THE LIVING WATER

BY

VICTORIA NALANI KNEUBUHL

First Commissioned

and Produced

by the Honolulu Theatre for Youth

"The man with the water gourd, he is a god,

water that causes the withered vine to flourish."

Kumulipo, Chant 1 ln. 112

Ka Wai Ola was first produced by the Honolulu Theatre for Youth at Leeward Community College Theatre on January 12, 1998. The production was directed by Kati Kuroda with the following cast:

KEANU . . . . .Nathan C.K. Mark
LIKO, etc. . . . . .Kyle Kakuno
HEALANI, MĀLIE, etc. . . . . .Cynthia See
GINA, etc. . . . . .Sheilah Sealey
ENSEMBLE . . . . .Daryl Bonilla and Walter Eccles

Set Design: Don Yanik
Light Design: Richard Schaefer
Costume Design: Casey Cameron Dinmore
Choreographer: Vicky Holt Takamine
Sound Design: Darin Au

CAST:

KEANU

LIKO / KUPUNA KĀNE

HEALANI

MĀLIE, KUPUNA WAHINE, MA (voice only)

GINA, YOUNG HAWAIIAN GIRL / YOUNG HEALANI / ʻOʻOPU NĀKEA /
    SISTERFISH

Ensemble 1: MICHAEL WOOLER / BOY 1 / PALIKŪ / KĀNE /
    FOREIGNER 2 / JORGEN JORGENSON / HĀLOA 1 / SANTINO /
    PA, POLICEMAN 1 / VOICE

Ensemble 2: BOY 2 / DOCTOR / MAHINA / KONOHIKI / KANALOA /
    LONDON NEWSKID / FOREIGNER 1 / E.K. BULL / HĀLOA 2 /
    DON PARASINO / PIO / POLICEMAN 2

SET: A house, loʻi, a stream, and a free playing area to
        accommodate all other locations.

TIME: Now and Before.

Kyle Kakuno, Walter Eccles, Nathan Mark.

SCENE 1

(LIKO works in the loʻi. HEALANI and KEANU are in the house.)

KEANU: *(looking at LIKO)* What's he doing out there?

HEALANI: He's fixing up the old loʻi, to grow taro again.

KEANU: Mom, he's so weird—

HEALANI: Keanu . . .

KEANU: This morning, before it's even light, he's going—*(takes a small gourd and does a nonsense chant)*

HEALANI: Be careful with my gourd. *(takes the gourd away from KEANU)*

KEANU: Sorry.

HEALANI: Someone special gave it to me. I was younger than you.

KEANU: I was showing you what he did.

HEALANI: Give him a chance, he just got here.

KEANU: Well, how long is the guy staying?

HEALANI: The guy is my uncle, Tūtū's brother. He's your Uncle Liko, and we're the only family he has left.

KEANU: Just our luck.

HEALANI: I was just a little girl when he ran—when he disappeared.

KEANU: Why did he?

HEALANI: It was around the time that Tūtū and I . . . that we had to leave here. He just, well, he just left. Anyway, I don't remember.

KEANU: But why?

HEALANI: I don't know why. But he's been living alone in the back of some valley on Molokaʻi all these years. He's bound to be different. Hurry up, you'll be late for school.

KEANU: Don't forget the cake for tomorrow.

HEALANI: Cake?

KEANU: For the soccer awards picnic, remember? You told me to sign up for dessert.

HEALANI: I'm sorry Keanu, but tomorrow I—I have something really important to do.

KEANU: Mom, I'm getting a trophy and everything.

HEALANI: Look, I'll get you a cake and you can take Uncle Liko.

KEANU: Get real! I'm not going out in public with him! You hardly came to any of my games. You promised!

HEALANI: You know how the ditch company wants to move the water from our stream to the other side?

KEANU: *(to himself)* How could I possibly forget?

HEALANI: Well, tomorrow they're going to try to do it.

KEANU: So?

HEALANI: Our group, Mālama Pono, is blocking off the road, and then we're going to stand there at the gate to the water tunnel so they can't get in.

KEANU: So you might get arrested again.

HEALANI: They're stealing our water.

KEANU: You know what people say about you?

HEALANI: What?

KEANU: That you just want to make trouble. That you don't really care about what other people want.

HEALANI: Why? Because our group won't give in and let the ditch company build us a Recreation Center?

KEANU: Everyone could use the Center. Only taro farmers use the water.

HEALANI: That Center is a bribe to make us all shut up!

KEANU: What's so great about some roots in the mud?

(HEALANI and KEANU hold.)

SCENE 2

(LIKO works in the loʻi. GINA enters.)

GINA: Hi. I'm Gina.

LIKO: Aloha.

GINA: Are you Uncle Liko?

LIKO: ʻAe.

GINA: Did you really stay in that valley for years and years all by yourself?

LIKO: You know what's nīele?

GINA: Yeah.

LIKO: What?

GINA: Nosey. But I can't help it if I'm curious. Are you planting kalo? Could I help?

LIKO: Come. Watch me. Do like I do. This the—

GINA: I know, the huli, the baby plant.

LIKO: This is from the makua—

GINA: The parent stalk.

LIKO: That's right, these are their children. Now plant the huli inside the mud. Yeah, push the mud around, just enough so the huli can hold on.

(*LIKO and GINA plant huli.*)

GINA: I just moved here.

LIKO: How come you know so much about kalo if you just move here?

GINA: My father told me. This valley is all he used to talk about. He told me everything about it, over and over again. All he ever wanted was to come back here to live.

LIKO: I guess he missed it.

GINA: He's Hawaiian, and he missed it so much. He taught me a lot of things, like hula and how to make lei. And he told me stories too. But mostly he talked about this valley and the things that happened here.

LIKO: Yeah? I used to live here, long time ago, too.

GINA: We were in a big city. There were hardly any plants there.

LIKO: Too bad.

GINA: I hope I never have to leave here. (*pause*) Why did you?

LIKO: What?

GINA: Leave here.

LIKO: To get away.

GINA: Then why did you come back?

LIKO: There was something—I thought I could . . .

(Focus on HEALANI and KEANU. LIKO watches.)

KEANU: Why did we have to come and live in the middle of mud holes and mosquitoes anyway?

HEALANI: Keanu, we were cheated out of this land. This is our family home. I worked so hard to get it back.

KEANU: So you got what you want.

HEALANI: It's for you too.

KEANU: You never ask me what I want.

HEALANI: I know you've had to give some things up.

KEANU: Yeah, like my father.

HEALANI: That's different. He—

KEANU: He what?

HEALANI: Nothing.

KEANU: Why can't you come tomorrow?

HEALANI: I promised Mālama Pono I—

KEANU: Mālama Pono. Mālama Pono. I'm sick of Mālama Pono. And I'm sick of all those meetings at our house. I'm sick of always seeing your picture in the paper at some stupid protest. And I'm sick of kids making fun of me! I bet that's why my father left, isn't it?

HEALANI: No! You don't understand! When you're older it will—

KEANU: When I'm older I'm getting as far away from this valley and as far away from you as I can! *(exits the house and enters the loʻi)*

LIKO: Aloha kakahiaka, ē Keanu.

KEANU: *(ignores him)* Let's go, Gina.

GINA: *(to KEANU)* Have you got the frogs?

LIKO: *(chuckles, to GINA)* What? You need frogs for go school?

GINA: Yeah, see we have to do this gross science project, and we—

KEANU: *(irritated)* I've got them, Gina. Now let's get out of here.

GINA: *(to LIKO)* Bye.

LIKO: Aloha.

KEANU: *(as they exit)* He's so weird.

GINA: Yeah, like me.

KEANU: No way.

GINA: That's how everyone at school treats me, 'cause I'm new.

KEANU: People treat me funny sometimes.

GINA: Really?

KEANU: Because of my mom.

GINA: I was wondering, would you eat lunch with me today? You know, just so the other kids would see me eating with someone. They'd start to think I was okay. Could you help me?

KEANU: Sure.

GINA: Really, promise?

KEANU: Yeah, I promise.

SCENE 3

(In the lo'i, HEALANI is helping LIKO plant the huli. Enter MICHAEL WOOLER, a business type.)

MICHAEL: Ms. Taylor, Healani Taylor.

HEALANI: *(turning around)* Yes.

MICHAEL: It's you.

HEALANI: Me?

MICHAEL: You went to Stevenson Intermediate. I lived near you on Liholiho Street.

HEALANI: Your face looks—

MICHAEL: It's Michael, Michael Wooler. It was eighth grade and—

HEALANI: You're the boy who spent hours doing your Laurel and Hardy routines for me.

MICHAEL: This is a fine mess you've gotten us into this time, Stanley.

HEALANI: Then you made me watch all those old Bogart movies over and over so I could help you memorize the scenes.

MICHAEL: Gee, it's great to see you again. You look wonderful.

HEALANI: You too.

MICHAEL: Oh, thanks . . .

HEALANI: Well, so . . . hi, after twenty years! What are you doing here?

MICHAEL: Oh! Well, actually, I, uh, see, I didn't realize it was— Well, no one called you Healani then. I was sent. I don't know if I would have come. I mean I would if—I mean if I wasn't sent by, see, I work for—

HEALANI: For?

MICHAEL: The Oʻahu Ditch Company.

HEALANI: Oh, that nice company who forced my family off this land when I was a little girl?

MICHAEL: But they bought that land in good faith . . .

HEALANI: Don't kid yourself. They used a land deed with a phony signature. They used it to get us evicted.

MICHAEL: I was only seven years old then. I don't know anything about it, really.

HEALANI: Our family fell apart.

MICHAEL: It was way before my time.

HEALANI: We can learn a lot from the past, Michael.

MICHAEL: Hey, your eyes still flash green when you're mad.

HEALANI: And you still believe everything men in suits tell you!

MICHAEL: You know, I feel really weird about this. Maybe I should get someone else to come out.

HEALANI: Look, it's okay, just tell me what they want.

MICHAEL: They just want me to talk to you.

HEALANI: About?

MICHAEL: About your group not wanting to share the water.

HEALANI: Share! Share?

MICHAEL: Can you not yell like that? You're making me nervous.

HEALANI: How can you talk about sharing? They built that tunnel and stole the water from this stream.

MICHAEL: They moved the water to grow sugarcane, to make jobs. People got to make a living, buy a house, raise families.

HEALANI: Well, there's no sugarcane now, so we'll just keep the water, thanks.

MICHAEL: Having water means having the possibility of growth, and growth means work. Maybe there's no cane, but people still need jobs, they still need to make a living and feed their families.

HEALANI: You're talking about development.

MICHAEL: It's not a dirty word. *(pause)* Be realistic. Can't you see you're holding back a valuable resource?

HEALANI: Can't you see I'm protecting the environment?

MICHAEL: But we have to look at the big picture.

HEALANI: What if I look at that picture and see you there, using recycled water?

MICHAEL: I'd say you didn't check the price tag.

HEALANI: So your company thinks it's cheaper to ruin an ecosystem?

MICHAEL: Sometimes we're just forced into making hard choices.

HEALANI: So we choose what means the most to us. *(short pause)* Why did you really come here?

MICHAEL: They want me to—remember, I'm just the messenger—

HEALANI: I remember.

MICHAEL: They know you're a single mother with a really bright son, one who could get into a private school, a good mainland college. They know how much money you make, and—

HEALANI: *(smiling)* And if I could just see my way clear to changing my position about the water, they'd be glad to help us out?

MICHAEL: If I'd known it was you I would have told them not to bother. I remember how you were about stray dogs and lost causes.

HEALANI: Michael, this will never be a lost cause.

MICHAEL: Well, here we are on different sides of the stream, huh?

HEALANI: I guess.

MICHAEL: Maybe I'll see you around sometime.

HEALANI: Maybe.

MICHAEL: Bye.

(*MICHAEL exits. HEALANI watches.*)

LIKO: You sure know how for talk.

HEALANI: When I had to prove that signature was phony, I learned . . .

(*LIKO is stung by this remark, but HEALANI is too preoccupied to notice.*)

HEALANI: You know, sometimes I think maybe I'm not a very good mother.

LIKO: Maybe, better I never come back.

HEALANI: I know I've made it hard for Keanu.

LIKO: Maybe I make it hard for everybody.

HEALANI: See, I wanted it to be for him too. I thought someday he would feel—like part of something. But maybe it's just me who cares.

LIKO: When the man came, I remember—

HEALANI: You know the kids at school, sometimes they—

(*LIKO and HEALANI hold.*)

SCENE 4

(*KEANU and GINA about to eat lunch at school.*)

GINA: Thanks for doing this, Keanu.

KEANU: Um, so where do you want to sit?

GINA: Maybe over there by—

(Enter BOY 1 and BOY 2.)

BOY 1: Hey look, there's Mr. Activist.

BOY 2: Yeah. Keanu, where's your protest sign?

BOY 1: Hey, why you no go live Kahoʻolawe?

BOY 2: And let us have our rec center?

BOY 1: Or next time, go stay in jail with your mom.

GINA: *(to KEANU)* Don't listen to them. *(to BOYS)* Civil
disobedience isn't a crime, you know.

BOY 1: Oh, big words. Yeah, Gina?

BOY 2: Yeah, "fresh off the boat." You think you better than us?

BOY 1: *(threatening)* So what, Keanu?

BOY 2: *(threatening)* You no like us have rec center?

BOY 1: Sports field?

KEANU: *(getting tough too)* Hey, I told you. I don't believe that
stupid stuff, like my mother!

BOY 1: *(like a pal)* Eh, no get fractured, brah.

BOY 2: Yeah, we just testing you.

KEANU: *(mirrors them)* Yeah . . . yeah, I knew that.

BOY 1: We know you one of us.

KEANU: *(brightens)* Yeah, right.

BOY 2: So come on, let's go eat lunch.

KEANU: Well, I—

(BOYS move KEANU away from GINA.)

BOY 1: So what? You rather hang out with Miss F-O-B?

KEANU: *(going to get his things)* Uh, sorry Gina, I forgot. I promised to eat lunch with these guys.

GINA: You mean you're just going to leave?

KEANU: *(moving away)* Look, we can do this some other day.

> *(Lights fade on GINA as the BOYS exit. Focus moves to LIKO and HEALANI.)*

HEALANI: It just isn't worth it, not if means my son hates me.

LIKO: Maybe I make it worse.

HEALANI: No, no. It's nothing to do with you, Uncle Liko.

LIKO: Maybe everything to do with me.

HEALANI: No, Uncle, it's not your fault.

LIKO: He not even calling me Uncle.

HEALANI: Wherever I am, you're always welcome, Uncle Liko. Eh, I'm late. I have to go help Mālama Pono. This might be the last thing I do for them. See you when I get back.

LIKO: Yeah, when you get back.

SCENE 5

> *(HEALANI sits on a bench. On the opposite side of the stage, KEANU is sitting at a desk.)*

HEALANI: I was in the truck.

KEANU: I was at school.

HEALANI: I was going to help block the road. We were using boulders.

KEANU: We were going to start the science project. We were using frogs.

HEALANI: The men loaded up the truck with really big rocks.

KEANU: I had a little one in a glass jar.

HEALANI: I was driving up the valley road—

KEANU: I was looking at the little frog—

HEALANI: I was thinking about all the times I left him alone.

KEANU: It was looking back at me with big eyes—

HEALANI: I was trying to figure out a way to—

KEANU: I was feeling like it knew—

HEALANI: I was hoping it wasn't too late to—

KEANU: It was making me sick to think that—

HEALANI: I think I took the turn too fast.

KEANU: The teacher was pouring chloroform on the cotton—

HEALANI: The boulders in the truck shifted all at once—

KEANU: She stuck it in the jar and the frog began to—

HEALANI: I was spinning off the road.

KEANU: I felt like I couldn't breathe, I—

HEALANI: I felt it roll, I—

KEANU: I felt the room spinning around—

HEALANI: I was screaming—

KEANU: Faster and faster—

HEALANI: Keanu!

KEANU and **HEALANI:** Then everything went black.

SCENE 6

(HEALANI lies down on the bench covered with a sheet as if on a hospital bed. A DOCTOR stands over her. LIKO and KEANU enter.)

DOCTOR: Only a few minutes.

KEANU: What's the—

DOCTOR: She's lost a lot of blood.

KEANU: Will she—

DOCTOR: I don't know.

KEANU: When will you—

DOCTOR: Come back tomorrow.

KEANU: But—

DOCTOR: She needs quiet and rest. Come back tomorrow.

(LIKO and KEANU turn to meet PALIKŪ.)

PALIKŪ: Hey, Keanu!

(KEANU turns away.)

LIKO: Keanu, you know him?

KEANU: I know him.

LIKO: Say hello.

(KEANU turns away.)

PALIKŪ: *(to LIKO)* I'm Palikū, Healani's friend from Mālama Pono. You must be Uncle Liko.

LIKO: Aloha.

PALIKŪ: I came to tell you we're sorry about Healani, about the accident. Everyone at Mālama Pono, we want you to know, if there's anything we can—

KEANU: *(flipping out)* You did this to her. You and your stupid protest. Get away. Get away from her. I hate you, and I hate Mālama Pono! *(runs away)*

LIKO: *(shaking his head)* Excuse him. He's having hard time.

SCENE 7

(Night. LIKO is near the house.)

LIKO: *(calling)* Keanu! Keanu! Eh, Keanu!

GINA: *(entering)* Did he come back?

LIKO: No.

GINA: Oh-oh.

LIKO and GINA: Keanu! Keanu!

(PALIKŪ, MĀLIE, and MAHINA enter.)

PALIKŪ: What's wrong?

LIKO: It's the boy.

GINA: He ran away.

LIKO: Getting dark now.

GINA: Maybe you should call the police.

PALIKŪ: No, wait, let's look first, then if we can't find him—Oh, Liko, this is Mālie and Mahina from Mālama Pono.

LIKO: Aloha.

PALIKŪ: Let's spread out and look around here first.

GINA: I have a flashlight.

MĀLIE: Then come with me.

> *(Everyone searches and calls. MĀLIE and GINA end up near the loʻi.)*

GINA: Maybe we won't find him.

MĀLIE: It's really dark now.

GINA: What's that?

MĀLIE: I don't know. Shine the light.

GINA: Where is it?

MĀLIE: Over there.

> *(The flashlight shows KEANU.)*

GINA: Keanu, it's you . . .

MĀLIE: Keanu!

KEANU: *(surly)* What?

GINA: *(calling)* We found him! We found Keanu!

MAHINA: Where? Where are you?

MĀLIE: He's over here near the loʻi!

MAHINA: *(enters)* There you are.

> *(LIKO and PALIKŪ enter, and everyone gathers around KEANU.)*

LIKO: Keanu, I was looking all over for you.

KEANU: So now you found me.

PALIKŪ: What happened to your mother today—

KEANU: Don't any of you talk to me about my mother! You don't know anything about her!

LIKO: She was worried about you.

KEANU: Me? Look what she's done. Now she might—

> *(KEANU stops. He looks at LIKO and looks away.)*

KEANU: If she wasn't so crazy—

LIKO: What?

KEANU: You heard me! All of you are cracked, crazy, pupule!

LIKO: Tsā!

KEANU: Her and you and this stupid valley, the stupid water, stupid bay, stupid taro—

LIKO: *(yelling)* Stupid boy! You know how come? How come she's like that?

KEANU: Because she can't . . . because none of you can just leave things alone.

LIKO: *(walking away)* Ah, you waste time kid. What you know?

KEANU: I know how to walk away!

> *(LIKO stops, frozen, then slowly turns back, mad.)*

LIKO: *(slow, even)* Oh no, boy, you don't know nothing about walking away.

> *(LIKO moves away. MĀLAMA PONO confers.)*

GINA: *(to KEANU)* How come you're doing this?

KEANU: Shut up, Gina. It's not your mother.

> *(MĀLAMA PONO goes to LIKO.)*

MĀLIE: What do you want to do, Liko?

LIKO: The kid so pa'akikī—

PALIKŪ: Hey, come on, he's having hard time.

MĀLIE: His mother might—

MAHINA: And his father—right after the kid was born, he ran out.

MĀLIE: He told Healani he wasn't ready to be a father.

LIKO: So what I going do?

MĀLIE: You cannot just leave him.

LIKO: He like fight with everybody. He even yelling at Healani today. He no like me, he no like you, he no like nothing about this valley, where he come from, nothing.

PALIKŪ: 'Cause he doesn't know. He never know what happen here.

MĀLIE: I kept telling Healani she should talk to him.

PALIKŪ: She always like protect him.

MAHINA: Yeah, but somebody should tell him.

MĀLIE: So he knows why his mother does what she does.

PALIKŪ: Why we do things.

LIKO: Waste time talk to him.

PALIKŪ: Not waste time, Liko. Who we doing this for? Why bother if there's no more keiki who care?

MĀLIE: He needs to know about this valley and the people.

MAHINA: We need every one of our children to know.

MĀLIE: They're the ones who'll take our places.

PALIKŪ: You help us. You know how it was.

MAHINA: You know what happened!

LIKO: No, I no like—

MĀLIE: Please, do it for Healani.

LIKO: *(beat)* Okay, okay.

PALIKŪ: Good, let's go talk to him.

(*ALL move to KEANU.*)

LIKO: Keanu, we know you scared about your mother, but if you knew about this valley—

PALIKŪ: They're some things we know she wants you to know.

LIKO: How about we tell you a story about what happened?

KEANU: How about if you just get out of my life?

LIKO: *(mad again)* Is that what you like?

KEANU: Yeah!

LIKO: Okay!

KEANU: What do you mean, okay?

LIKO: You listen, and then after, if you like I go, I just go live somewhere else.

KEANU: Are you serious?

LIKO: I not fooling . . .

KEANU: You'll really go?

LIKO: Yeah, I go.

KEANU: Okay. So tell me. I'll listen.

PALIKŪ: Okay, first we gotta get some things.

(*PALIKŪ and MAHINA exit.*)

GINA: I think I better go now.

MĀLIE: No, Gina, we need you.

GINA: I really think I—

KEANU: Gina!

(KEANU motions GINA to come.)

KEANU: You can't leave me with these freaks.

GINA: You told me to shut up!

KEANU: Okay, sorry.

GINA: And you ditched me at school!

KEANU: Okay, okay, I'm sorry. Just don't leave me with them. Please . . . look, they could be *(makes the crazy sign)*. You wouldn't want anything to happen to me, would you?

GINA: *(rolls her eyes)* Okay. I'll stay.

> *(Enter PALIKŪ and MAHINA with two bundles of found objects that become props for the story.)*

MĀLIE: Gina, come.

GINA: *(to herself)* I'm such a sap.

PALIKŪ: Okay, we're almost ready.

> *(MAHINA plays a nose flute. Palikū beats the ipu. MĀLIE now becomes KUPUNA WAHINE. She and GINA walk in the stream with fishing baskets.)*

PALIKŪ: This is the beginning, before strangers came here. When everyone lived and worked in the valley, and the valley and the bay gave us everything, everything we needed.

MĀLIE and **GINA:** *(singing)*
'Ōpae li'ili'i
Little hihiwai
'O'opu nākea
Why are you so shy?
Swim into our basket
It is dark and cool
'O'opu nākea
Hiding in the pool.

'Ōpae li'ili'i
Little hihiwai
'O'opu nākea
Do you wonder why?
The sky is blue
And the trees are green.
'O'opu nākea
Swimming in the stream.

PALIKŪ: See, the women fished in the stream and down on the beach. They gathered food, wove mats, and the men worked in the lo'i, growing kalo.

KEANU: You mean I have to work too?

LIKO: Yeah, so you can do something besides moan.

(*LIKO and KEANU work in the lo'i.*)

LIKO: Look, see, the huli are planted. The first leaves are coming. Now, we drain the lo'i, let the ground dry little bit so the young roots have a chance to grab on tight to the soil. (*pause*) The first human born was Hāloanaka. He died and was buried, and from his body, up grew kalo. Then another human was born. His name was Hāloa, the first person. We are the children, children born from Hāloa. But kalo, Hāloanaka, he will always be our older brother.

(*MĀLIE, GINA, and MAHINA play the 'ukulele and sing while LIKO and KEANU work.*)

LIKO: Hele mai ke konohiki. The konohiki—

KEANU: I know, he's from the chief. I do go to school.

LIKO: Aloha ē, Konohiki.

KONOHIKI: Aloha nō, Liko. You have enough water?

LIKO: 'Ae, yes we do.

KONOHIKI: Down the valley, the stream washed branches into the ʻauwai! Water can't flow into the loʻi! The people need our help!

LIKO: Aloha ʻino! Let's help them clean it.

KONOHIKI: Tomorrow, we need a lot of hands.

LIKO: Of course we help. No water, no kalo.

KONOHIKI: No kalo, no food.

LIKO: Tomorrow then.

KONOHIKI: I ka lā ʻapōpō.

<u>SCENE 8</u>

(Evening.)

KUPUNA WAHINE: Mai, mai, it's night, come and lie down. Now is the time for rest.

> *(KUPUNA WAHINE walks to meet LIKO and KEANU. She takes KEANU by the hand. GINA plays a young Hawaiian girl. LIKO takes her aside.)*

LIKO: Baby! I have something for you.

GINA: What is it?

> *(LIKO reveals the water gourd from <u>SCENE 1</u>.)*

GINA: A water gourd.

LIKO: So you remember, baby. Water, water is life. Everything we love needs the water. You remember and take care. Mālama pono.

GINA: I'll remember.

*(KEANU has watched this exchange, and looks
sad for second.)*

KUPUNA WAHINE: You've had a hard day, haven't you?

KEANU: Yes.

KUPUNA WAHINE: Here, we're all together and well, Keanu. So you
rest.

GINA: Maybe Keanu would like to hear the story, the one about
Kāne.

(The sound of the nose flute and pahu.)

KUPUNA WAHINE: Aia ihea ka wai a Kāne? Kāne is a god who sends
the rain to fall on the earth. He makes the streams flow
with water. The water feeds the land and makes the kalo
grow, and the kalo feeds our people. Kāne is a god, but
when he chooses to dwell in the body of a man, he lives
in the beautiful land of Kānehunamoku, a hidden island
that floats in and out of sight. Sometimes at sunrise or at
sunset the island passes by.

*(In the dark, PALIKŪ and MAHINA flicker the
flashlights as they move around. They make
the sound of the wind and the soft sound of
crowing.)*

LIKO: Lights flicker from Kānehunamoku. Cocks crow and pigs
grunt and figures move about like shadows.

*(PALIKŪ and MAHINA stand as KĀNE and
KANALOA.)*

KUPUNA WAHINE: There lives Kāne, with his friend, the god
Kanaloa.

KĀNE: Here we drink ʻawa.

KANALOA: Here we eat food from the ever-growing garden.

KĀNE: The streams flow with the clearest waters.

KANALOA: This is a land of no sickness.

KĀNE: And no death.

KUPUNA WAHINE: For on that island is a pool of crystal water.

> *(A special light indicates a pool of water in the stream. KUPUNA WAHINE takes KEANU by the hand to the pool.)*

KUPUNA WAHINE: Come, Keanu, come . . .

> *(GINA hands the gourd filled with water to KEANU. He drinks.)*

LIKO: There, flowers always bloom, and birds sing.

KĀNE: Whoever drinks this water is always young.

KANALOA: Whoever drinks this water is made well.

KĀNE: Whoever is touched with this water will be restored to life.

KĀNE and **KANALOA:** Ka Wai Ola A Kāne.

> *(KĀNE and KANALOA fade.)*

GINA: That's how it was.

KEANU: So what happened?

GINA: That's how it was until they came. And some of the kūpuna saw. They saw everything that was coming.

SCENE 9

> *(Night. They settle down for sleep. KUPUNA WAHINE turns, dreaming. KEANU watches.)*

KUPUNA WAHINE: *(makes small dream noises)* Uhhh. Uh.

(*MAHINA becomes the* LONDON NEWSKID. *He
has an obnoxious cockney accent.* KUPUNA
WAHINE *hears him and sits up staring.*)

LONDON NEWSKID:
>London Daily!
>London Daily!
>Ladies and Gents
>Gents and Ladies
>Read this, read this!
>If you can read at all, that is.
>It's 1778, January 1778
>Cap'n Cook, Cap'n Cook
>'as found some islands he 'as
>found some islands
>an named 'em sandwich
>Sandwich Islands!
>Ladies and Gents
>Gents and Ladies.

KUPUNA WAHINE: Auē! I hear it—a terrible sound.

NEWSKID: An why does he call 'em sandwich, you might ask?
Cause the savages there likes to eat sandwiches, I 'eard, I
did.

KUPUNA WAHINE: Like horrible screeching.

NEWSKID: Cap'n Cook and 'is savage sandwich eating islands.
Ladies and gents, gents and ladies, read this, read
this! *(exits)*

KUPUNA WAHINE: *(waking)* No, no, stop it, no!

GINA: Kupuna, what is it?

KUPUNA WAHINE: Something, something that will change
everything, forever.

LIKO: That was only the first thing.

KEANU: *(to Gina)* We can't help it if that happened. The rest of the world was going to find us sooner or later.

SCENE 10

(Dressed like quirky nineteenth-century men, MAHINA and PALIKŪ step forward as FOREIGNER 1 and FOREIGNER 2. They admire each other.)

FOREIGNER 1: Now don't you look smashing.

FOREIGNER 2: I've heard these islands are absolutely smashing. Good place to make a killing. Oops, I mean a dollar.

FOREIGNER 1: Capital, simply capital.

FOREIGNER 2: Of course, there's the natives to deal with.

FOREIGNER 1: Not to worry. Just follow my lead.

FOREIGNER 2: Ah, you've had experience?

FOREIGNER 1: Quite.

FOREIGNER 2: *(bowing)* Then by all means, after you.

FOREIGNER 1: We're great new men upon your shore.

FOREIGNER 2: And we know so much more.

FOREIGNER 1 and **FOREIGNER 2:** *(clapping)* Hey, hey, hey, listen here.

> *(The sound of an ipu begins slowly and builds. Additional sounds of the ʻulīʻulī and kālaʻau join in and reach a frantic pace. The FOREIGNERS do a rhythmic dance routine.)*

FOREIGNER 1: Living like this isn't good.

FOREIGNER 2: Let us tell you how you should.

FOREIGNER 1: Wear more clothes.

FOREIGNER 2: Learn to pray.

FOREIGNER 1: Better change your native ways.

FOREIGNER 2: Cook and sew.

FOREIGNER 1: Read and write.

FOREIGNER 2: Work for money—

FOREIGNER 1 and **FOREIGNER 2:** Day and night.

FOREIGNER 1: Native chiefs are like cement.

FOREIGNER 2: You need our way of government.

FOREIGNER 1: Divide your land.

FOREIGNER 2: Just like we do.

FOREIGNER 1: That way we can have some too.

FOREIGNER 2: It was yours, now it's mine.

FOREIGNER 1: Sign along the dotted line.

FOREIGNER 2: If they always feel confused.

FOREIGNER 1: They won't notice what they lose.

>   *(The FOREIGNERS get rough. They push and shove the others.)*

FOREIGNER 1 and **FOREIGNER 2:** Tow the line, make the mark
      We'll tell you when to stop and start.

KEANU: Hey, stop shoving.

FOREIGNER 1 and **FOREIGNER 2:** We'll start selling
      We'll start growing
      You'll start buying
      You'll start owing.

FOREIGNER 1: Watch your world go round and round.

FOREIGNER 2: First you're up.

FOREIGNER 1: And then you're down.

KEANU: Leave me alone.

FOREIGNER 2: First you're north.

FOREIGNER 1: Then you're east.

FOREIGNER 1 and **FOREIGNER 2:** Now we're the most—

FOREIGNER 1: And you're—

FOREIGNER 2: The least.

KEANU: JUST LEAVE US ALONE!

FOREIGNER 1: No need to get so excited, young man.

FOREIGNER 2: We just came to do our best.

FOREIGNER 1 and **FOREIGNER 2:** So treat us like a welcome guest.

(The FOREIGNERS push everyone down.)

MĀLIE: Hey you guys are too rough!

MAHINA: Sorry.

PALIKŪ: I guess we got carried away.

(KEANU hesitates and goes to help LIKO up.)

LIKO: *(disgusted)* It's the same story all over! *(walks dejectedly to the lo'i. He sits.)*

KEANU: So, is this the end?

LIKO: What?

KEANU: Is this the end of the story?

LIKO: I wish.

KEANU: How much more?

LIKO: *(really grouchy)* No ask me.

KEANU: I'm getting tired.

LIKO: Yeah, we all tired, boy.

MĀLIE: Come on, Liko, you're still the Kupuna kāne.

LIKO: Yeah, yeah, I ready.

> *(GINA and KEANU stand near LIKO at the loʻi.)*

LIKO: Then comes the time to let the water back into the loʻi. All the huli had one chance for root. The ones that took root grow big and strong. The other ones, just too bad, nothing we can do.

KUPUNA WAHINE: *(entering)* Kupuna kāne, there's some men in the back of the valley, and they're buying up all the land.

> *(Silence. MĀLIE clears her throat, giving LIKO another cue.)*

KUPUNA WAHINE: *(louder)* I said, Kupuna kāne, the men are buying up—

LIKO: *(loud, irritated)* They not buying the land.

KUPUNA WAHINE: They're saying something about the water.

LIKO: *(louder)* They sign our names and say we sold it!

KUPUNA WAHINE: Uncle—

LIKO: *(yelling)* They sign our names on papers. They stealing!

KEANU: Quit yelling at her.

LIKO: Can't you see? I no like do this again!

MĀLIE: Uncle, uncle, it's okay, come, come sit down. Gina, take Keanu to Palikū and Mahina. Tell them I'll be there.

> *(MĀLIE sits and calms LIKO down.)*

LIKO: Sorry, I just no like remember.

MĀLIE: It's okay, it's okay, uncle.

(KEANU and GINA walk away.)

KEANU: Why don't we just get him a straightjacket?

GINA: I can see why you want to be friends with those boys at
school.

KEANU: What?

GINA: You sound just like them.

(KEANU stops and looks at her.)

GINA: Come on, I think they're over here.

SCENE 11

*(In the dark, PALIKŪ and MAHINA are laughing
as GINA and KEANU enter.)*

PALIKŪ: Where's Mālie?

GINA: She's coming.

PALIKŪ: Okay, so ready?

MAHINA: Ready.

*(The lights come on to reveal MAHINA as E. K.
BULL, dressed like a carnival barker, and PALIKŪ
as JORGEN JORGENSON, dressed for a safari.)*

BULL: I'm E. K. Bull, Oʻahu Ditch Company.

JORGEN: *(shaking BULL's hand)* I am Jorgen Jorgenson, engineer.

BULL: Let's talk water.

JORGEN: Ja, water.

BULL: See this stream, pouring fresh water in the sea? It's a waste.

JORGEN: Ja, big waste.

BULL: A few people grow taro.

JORGEN: Ja, only few.

BULL: That's what they use to make their poi, you know.

JORGEN: Ja, poi, ugh.

BULL: I'm buying up lots of land here to secure my rights.

JORGEN: Ja, rights.

BULL: We have to look at the future. We could take this water and turn it into hundreds of jobs.

JORGEN: Hundreds of jobs, ja.

BULL: If we take this water through the mountain to the central plain, we could grow thousands of acres of sugarcane.

JORGEN: Ja, thousands of acres.

BULL: It's about three miles to the other side.

JORGEN: *(considering)* Hmm, three miles, ja.

BULL: Don't lose faith now. I'd like you to blast me a water tunnel right through the mountain.

JORGEN: *(excited)* Blast? Oh ja!

BULL: Can you do it? Is it a go?

JORGEN: Ja! Ja! Ja! Go! Go! Go!

> *(JORGEN at work as E. K. BULL stands to one side, delivering his lines like a public relations speech.)*

BULL: The great feats of mankind
Are never forgotten

Ere mortals pass over
Our monuments remain.

(The others use the ipu, kāla'au, and pahu to make the rhythmic sounds of a construction site.)

JORGEN: We're digging and pounding
Breaking and shaking
Drilling and blasting.

BULL: We're building a tunnel.

JORGEN: We're whacking and thrusting
Moving and throwing
Pulling and pitching.

BULL: And we stand for progress.

JORGEN: We're pushing and shoving
Mawing and clawing
Ripping and tearing.

BULL: We're conquering nature for the greater good of all.

BULL and JORGEN: 10, 9, 8, 7, 6, 5, 4, 3, 2, 1.

(There is a loud blast followed by cheering and applause.)

JORGEN: I have finished! I have done it. I made a really big hole in the mountain!

SCENE 12

(GINA and KEANU return to MĀLIE and LIKO. They look in the stream.)

GINA: That's how the water in the stream got taken away.

MĀLIE: That's when it got really bad.

LIKO: They took everything.

MAHINA: Hardly any water came down the stream.

LIKO: Everything.

PALIKŪ: People couldn't grow kalo.

LIKO: We left with nothing.

MĀLIE: Or gather food from the stream.

LIKO: Nothing.

MAHINA: Every year, less fish in the bay.

LIKO: People had to move away. Everyone started to forget.

MĀLIE: *(singing)*

> I think there was a time
> when the valley streams were flowing
> I think there was a time
> full of fishes in the sea
> when the voices of the birds
> whose names we have forgotten
> were singing songs from every forest tree.
>
> And I think there was a time when
> the forest grew forever
> From the mountains
> just as far as you could see
> When the air was always fresh
> every rainbow arching morning
> with misty rain as gentle as can be.
>
> I think there was a time
> when families stayed together
> and everyone had room enough to share
> when no one had to sleep
> alone and unremembered

when everybody took the time to care
I know there is a way
to tell you what I'm feeling
In words that go beyond what you may fear
A way to touch those dreams
growing deep inside you
water them with care and you will hear
their song,
water them with care and you will hear.

KEANU: Everything has to change.

MĀLIE: But whose voice decides how things change?

KEANU: Not mine.

GINA: You said you didn't care about the kalo, or the stream, or the valley—

KEANU: I just said I didn't care.

GINA: So if you don't care, you decide to just let things happen.

KEANU: Not.

GINA: Yes.

KEANU: Not.

GINA: Yes.

> *(LIKO motions to KEANU and GINA to come near the loʻi.)*

LIKO: Eh, come, you kids come over here. Look, the time comes when the leaves of the kalo open up and grow out, strong, and the whole loʻi looks so green and pretty. The leaves come big like green hearts, moving and swaying when the wind blows by. Makes you feel good, you know.

MĀLIE: *(to MAHINA)* Ready?

MAHINA and **PALIKŪ:** Yeah.

GINA: *(to MĀLIE)* Is it now?

MĀLIE: Now!

> *(MĀLIE and GINA rush in on either side of KEANU. They spin him around. The stage goes dark. Weird lights and music.)*

SCENE 13

> *(When the lights rise, KEANU is squashed between PALIKŪ and MAHINA as HĀLOA 1 and HĀLOA 2, two giant kalo.)*

HĀLOA 1: Hey, kama, no wiggle.

KEANU: What are you doing? What are you?

HĀLOA 2: What we look like?

KEANU: Well, you look like—

HĀLOA 1 and **HĀLOA 2:** TWO BIG BUMBUCHA KALO!

HĀLOA 1: I'm Hāloanaka, that's my brother—

HĀLOA 2: I'm Hāloanaka, too.

HĀLOA 1 and **HĀLOA 2:** Twins!

KEANU: I'm—

HĀLOA 1: We know you.

HĀLOA 2: Yeah, our kid brother.

HĀLOA 1: Too bad you one brat.

KEANU: Hey, I'm not a—

HĀLOA 1 and **HĀLOA 2:** *(whacking KEANU with their butts)* Brat! Brat! Brat!

KEANU: Stop it!

HĀLOA 1: Eh, you never care about us.

HĀLOA 2: Yeah, "Who cares about some roots-in-the-mud?"

HĀLOA 1 and **HĀLOA 2:** Pretty rude, brah.

KEANU: Well, I didn't know before. That's it, I didn't know.

HĀLOA 1: Well you know now.

HĀLOA 2: And you going know more.

HĀLOA 1: See, us kalo, we have one goal in life.

HĀLOA 2: Yeah.

HĀLOA 1: To grow.

HĀLOA 2: Yeah, yeah, yeah, grow, grow, grow.

HĀLOA 1: And if we grow really good, we get to be—

HĀLOA 1 and **HĀLOA 2:** *(beatific)* Poi!

HĀLOA 1: But you! You no like us grow!

HĀLOA 2: Yeah, you dirty buggah.

HĀLOA 1: Yeah, you no like us have water!

HĀLOA 2: Yeah, how would you like no more water?

HĀLOA 1: You know what it's like?

KEANU: Ah, no.

HĀLOA 1: Like dis.

HĀLOA 2: We going show you.

(To the sound of agony music, the lights turn harsh and hard. The HĀLOAS squeeze KEANU between them.)

KEANU: *(trying to push on the HĀLOAS)* Can you move over? I'm too hot.

HĀLOA 1: Tough beans, kid.

KEANU: Come on.

HĀLOA 2: Eh, shut up, you kid-in-the-mud.

KEANU: Okay, I'm thirsty, I get it. We can stop.

HĀLOA 1: Stop? We only started.

HĀLOA 2: Feeling like you all crack up and dry?

KEANU: Yeah.

HĀLOA 1: Feeling rotten?

KEANU: Yeah.

HĀLOA 2: Like one dried out buffo body—

HĀLOA 1: On the road at noon?

KEANU: Yeah. Now gimme some water!

HĀLOA 1: Oh, sorry, sonny—

HĀLOA 2: Sorry, pally—

HĀLOA 1: No more water.

HĀLOA 2: Yeah, no more.

KEANU: Come on, please, I feel like I'm—like—

HĀLOA 1: That's what happens when you no more water—

HĀLOA 1 and **HĀLOA 2:** YOU DIE!

HĀLOA 1: I think he gets the pitcha—

HĀLOA: No. No give him the pitcha, give him—

HĀLOA 1 and **HĀLOA 2:** The Stream!

> *(The HĀLOAS twirl KEANU around and push him in the stream. Weird lights and the sound of a big splash.)*

SCENE 14

> *(GINA as 'O'OPU NĀKEA swims up to him and screams.)*

'O'OPU: I thought you were one of them. Are you?

KEANU: What are you supposed to be?

'O'OPU: 'O'opu. 'O'opu Nākea. If you're not one of them, better watch out.

KEANU: What are you talking about?

> *(PALIKŪ as the gangster parasite SANTINO swims in aggressively with an assault weapon, randomly firing around as he moves through the stream.)*

KEANU: What is that?

'O'OPU: A parasite. They all used to get washed away, down the stream. They're not very good swimmers, but now that there's not enough water to wash them away—watch out!

> *(SANTINO pops out, cruises around, and retreats.)*

'O'OPU: Not enough water. The stream's not strong enough, and the water's all dirty. They love it. So now they're moving in everywhere, killing anything that gets in their way. You better hide.

KEANU: What?

'O'OPU: I'm not kidding. I'm the last, the last one of my kind—

(SANTINO enters.)

'O'OPU: And I'm outta here.

(SANTINO viciously attacks and captures KEANU. SANTINO drags him to MAHINA as the Godfather parasite DON PARASINO. SANTINO kneels and kisses the DON's oversized ring.)

SANTINO: Godfather.

DON: Santino, my son, did you take care of that business?

SANTINO: I'm sorry, Godfather, she got away. I'm sorry, I don't have the pasta 'o'opu.

DON: Santino, now what have I told you?

SANTINO: I know, never give the Don bad news on an empty stomach. I'm sorry, so sorry.

(SANTINO weeps, cries, and moans profusely.)

DON: It's okay, Santino. You know you are like a son to me. The Don forgives you. Now get up. You embarrass me, Santino.

SANTINO: Godfather, I brought in the parasite who's trying to move in on our territory.

(SANTINO shoves KEANU down in front of the DON.)

KEANU: Hey, cut it out.

SANTINO: Aw, shut your face, scum.

DON: You're the worst sort of parasite, turning on your own kind. You disgust me.

KEANU: I'm not a parasite.

SANTINO: Don't lie to us. Now get on your knees and kiss the ring.

(*KEANU effusively kisses the DON's ring.*)

SANTINO: I said kiss it! Don't start a relationship with it.

DON: Oh, we've heard about you.

SANTINO: Yeah, mauka, makai, we heard.

DON: You don't want no more water in the stream.

SANTINO: That's what all us parasites want, less H_2O.

DON: And that's how we knows you're one of us.

SANTINO: 'Cause no way we want more water.

DON: Less H_2O means we never get washed into the ocean, capeesh?

SANTINO: So we can run all the action here.

DON: And you ain't muscling us out! Santino, help me up.

SANTINO: (*aside*) His home gym, he never uses it.

(*DON and SANTINO take KEANU by the arms.*)

DON: Baci di morte . . . You know what that means, son?

SANTINO: It means you ain't gonna score in our neighborhood.

DON: Come, let's take a walk.

SANTINO: Because you're going for a long swim in a short stream.

DON: You're gonna dive into the big one.

SANTINO: The waters of no return.

DON and **SANTINO:** The bay!

SCENE 15

(Weird lights and music mix with the sounds of crashing waves. KEANU whirls around and ends up under the ocean.)

KEANU: What next?

(GINA as SISTERFISH swims in. She looks KEANU over.)

SISTERFISH: What is this? Ma! Something strange floated in.

MA: *(offstage voice/MĀLIE)* You know what to do.

(SISTERFISH bites him.)

KEANU: Ouch, that hurts!

SISTERFISH: Ma! I don't know what is this.

MA: *(offstage)* What does it look like?

SISTERFISH: I never seen anything this ugly in the bay before!

KEANU: Wait a minute.

MA: *(offstage)* Taste it again. Make sure it isn't poison.

(SISTERFISH bites him again.)

KEANU: Ouch, stop it!

SISTERFISH: Tastes okay, but talks.

MA: *(offstage)* Call your brothers.

SISTERFISH: Pa! Pio!

(PALIKŪ and MAHINA as PA and PIO swim in.)

PA: Eh, what?

PIO: What?

PA: What?

PA and **PIO:** Sistah?

SISTERFISH: Look.

> *(PA and PIO check out KEANU.)*

PA: Hey wow.

PIO: Wow.

PA: Wow.

PA and **PIO:** Ono!

SISTERFISH: If you bite it, it talks.

> *(PA and PIO bite.)*

KEANU: Hey, stop it!

SISTERFISH: See?

KEANU: That hurts.

SISTERFISH: Eh, no can help. We—

PA: Starving.

PIO: Starving.

PA and **PIO:** Starving.

SISTERFISH: The stream used to wash things down to—

PA: Feed us.

PIO: Feed us.

PA and **PIO:** Feed us.

SISTERFISH: But now no more water, nothing washing down, no—

PA: Food.

PIO: Food.

PA and **PIO:** *(licking their chops at KEANU)* Food.

SISTERFISH: So instead of growing up we going—

PA: Make.

PIO: Die.

PA and **PIO:** Dead.

KEANU: Too bad!

SISTERFISH: *(pushes KEANU)* All that could change.

KEANU: If there was more stream water?

SISTERFISH: Or if—if we could find somebody, uh, something, to last for a lot of—

PA: Meals.

PIO: Meals.

PA and **PIO:** Meals.

KEANU: Meals?

SISTERFISH: You know, something really big for—

PA: Grind.

PIO: Grind.

PA and **PIO:** Grind.

SISTERFISH: Say, what are you doing for—

PA: Breakfast?

PIO: Lunch?

PA and **PIO:** And dinner?

(The fish attack KEANU in a feeding frenzy.)

KEANU: Hey, stop it, stop it, leave me alone! I said, get away from me! Leave me alone!

> *(After roughing him up a little, PALIKŪ and MAHINA back off.)*

SCENE 16

(GINA takes KEANU to one side.)

GINA: Are you all right?

KEANU: Yeah. I don't know why I have to listen to all of this.

GINA: You're lucky, Keanu.

KEANU: You think I'm lucky?

GINA: Lucky that people care enough to tell you. Even after . . .

KEANU: After the way I act?

> *(GINA just looks at him.)*

KEANU: I guess you think I'm a jerk.

GINA: Yeah, sometimes.

> *(MAHINA, PALIKŪ, MĀLIE and LIKO to one side.)*

LIKO: I no like.

MĀLIE: We have to—

LIKO: Why? Why you folks like to do that?

PALIKŪ: Because, he needs to see it.

GINA: I hope your mom's okay.

KEANU: Don't say it like that, Gina.

GINA: Like what?

KEANU: Like you think she's—like you think she might—

LIKO: *(interrupting)* Come, come look at the lo'i. Look what happen. All the leaves that was full, now they coming faded and pale. They look sick, like they going make. We work and work and looks like all the plants going die anyway, so might as well just give up, yeah?

SCENE 17

(MĀLIE is at the house as TŪTŪ.)

LIKO: Look, one more thing, one more thing they like show you. See, that's your grandmother there, Tūtū, my sister. Long time ago, we used to take care your mother together, see. Now watch this.

(LIKO enters the house.)

LIKO: My own sister, you don't believe me? I never sign the paper.

TŪTŪ: That was your name on top the deed, Liko.

LIKO: I told you I never!

TŪTŪ: Then how your name came there?

LIKO: I don't know. They cheating us.

TŪTŪ: Who? Who?

LIKO: Who you think? You know who wants this land!

TŪTŪ: But why?

LIKO: They no like us use water for kalo. They no like anybody get in the way.

TŪTŪ: Why don't you do something?

LIKO: What I going do?

TŪTŪ: Why you cannot get help?

LIKO: What kind help? Lawyer? Nobody going help us. They got all the money. Us, we no more money. We can not even put food in our mouths. How we going fight them?

TŪTŪ: They trying for steal our land.

LIKO: They good at stealing.

(GINA *enters as* YOUNG HEALANI.)

LIKO: Healani, what you doing here?

YOUNG HEALANI: Why are you yelling, Uncle Liko?

(Silence.)

YOUNG HEALANI: Mama, why are you yelling?

TŪTŪ: Nothing, it's nothing, baby, you go outside and play. Pretty soon I call you.

(YOUNG HEALANI *exits to the lo'i.*)

TŪTŪ: And her, what going happen to Healani when we no more place for live? You gotta do something.

LIKO: Me? Me? What I going do? I nothing.

TŪTŪ: Your name on top the paper, on the deed, Liko!

LIKO: Stop! I told you stop!

TŪTŪ: But get your name on top.

LIKO: What, what, you accusing me? You blame me? I told you I never sign the paper! You no believe me, my own sister? What, what you think I am?

TŪTŪ: I didn't mean—

LIKO: Okay, I doing something. I getting out!

TŪTŪ: What?

LIKO: You blaming me! I leaving!

TŪTŪ: No, Liko, you cannot just leave—

LIKO: You blame me!

TŪTŪ: No, no, I didn't—

LIKO: I getting as far away from this valley, as far away from you, as I can go.

TŪTŪ: *(grabs him)* No, Liko, sorry, please, please don't leave us here, sorry—

LIKO: *(pushes her away)* No, no touch me.

(LIKO storms out of the house.)

YOUNG HEALANI: Uncle Liko, where are you going?

LIKO: I gotta go away for a while now, baby.

YOUNG HEALANI: When are you coming back?

LIKO: I don't know.

YOUNG HEALANI: Look, I have the water gourd. I'll water the kalo until you come back.

LIKO: Yeah, good, you give the huli water.

YOUNG HEALANI: You won't be gone too long, will you?

LIKO: *(exiting)* You be a good girl, Healani.

(LIKO exits scene and goes to KEANU.)

KEANU: She said she didn't know why. She said she doesn't remember why . . .

LIKO: She remembers.

KEANU: You left them. You left my mother.

LIKO: I told you, boy, you don't know nothing about walking away. Now look—

> *(LIKO turns KEANU around to see YOUNG HEALANI watering the kalo with the water gourd. The light fades on YOUNG HEALANI and rises quickly in the house, where PALIKŪ and MAHINA as POLICEMAN 1 and POLICEMAN 2 are in a heated argument with TŪTŪ.)*

TŪTŪ: No, I not!

POLICEMAN 1: Look, you gotta get out, lady.

POLICEMAN 2: See, this is an eviction notice.

TŪTŪ: No, I no more place for go.

POLICEMAN 1: That's not our problem.

POLICEMAN 2: We're just doing our job.

POLICEMAN 1: You gotta leave.

TŪTŪ: This is our home! I not leaving.

POLICEMAN 1: Don't make us force you.

> *(The argument escalates to yelling.)*

TŪTŪ: I told you, I not leaving!

POLICEMAN 2: You have to!

POLICEMAN 1: We can arrest you!

TŪTŪ: I not going!

POLICEMAN 2: *(moving to grab her)* You are!

> *(They struggle. POLICEMAN 2 grabs her.)*

POLICEMAN 2: We're just doing our job.

TŪTŪ: *(breaks free)* I not. I not.

POLICEMAN 2: Grab her!

> *(POLICEMAN 1 grabs TŪTŪ.)*

TŪTŪ: Let go! Let go of me! I not going! I not going!

> *(YOUNG HEALANI runs in.)*

YOUNG HEALANI: What are you doing? What are you doing?

> *(YOUNG HEALANI kicks and beats on POLICEMAN 1.)*

TŪTŪ: You take our water, now you take our land.

YOUNG HEALANI: Stop! Stop! You're hurting her.

TŪTŪ: This our home! We one family!

POLICEMAN 1: Grab the kid. Grab the kid.

> *(POLICEMAN 2 grabs YOUNG HEALANI and pulls her away.)*

YOUNG HEALANI: Don't hurt her. Don't you hurt my Mama.

> *(TUTU and YOUNG HEALANI hold on to parts of the house. The POLICEMEN try to pull them out.)*

TŪTŪ: No you can't, you can't make us.

YOUNG HEALANI: Leave her alone. Leave us alone.

TŪTŪ: We not leaving. We not.

YOUNG HEALANI: Mama! Mama!

TŪTŪ: Hang on, hang on baby. Don't let them. Try to hang on.

YOUNG HEALANI: Why? Why are you doing this? We never hurt you. We never hurt you.

TŪTŪ: We not leaving. We not leaving. We not. We not.

YOUNG HEALANI: Stop. Stop. Stop it!

(KEANU runs into the scene and starts hitting POLICEMAN 2.)

KEANU: Leave her alone. You leave her alone. I'll kill you. You leave her alone!!

LIKO: *(voice breaks in over their screams)* No! That's enough. Pau! No more. This is no good. No use already. Enough!

(Everyone turns to look at LIKO.)

LIKO: *(to KEANU)* I leaving, tomorrow. Better I never came back. Like you want, I leaving. No use I stay. *(broken, turns to walk away)*

KEANU: Wait . . . Uncle Liko . . . wait.

LIKO: What? What you call me?

KEANU: I said . . . Uncle Liko . . . I . . .

LIKO: What? What you want from me? *(pause)* I just one old man now. *(starts away again)*

KEANU: No, wait, Uncle Liko, come back.

(A special light returns us to the pool in the stream as in the KĀNE story. KEANU moves to LIKO and takes his hand.)

KEANU: Don't go, Uncle Liko. Stay with us.

(KEANU takes LIKO to the pool, and fills the water gourd for LIKO, who drinks. LIKO hands the gourd to KEANU who also drinks.)

PALIKŪ: Whoever drinks of this water—

MAHINA: Is made well.

GINA: Whoever drinks of this water—

MĀLIE: Is restored to life. *(walks to LIKO)* Tell us, Uncle Liko, tell us all the last thing.

(Everyone follows LIKO to the lo‘i.)

LIKO: You see now, just when the kalo looks like it's dying, when the leaves go brown and curl up, don't give up. Because inside, under the ground, the kalo is growing, really growing big and strong to feed us all, to give us life, so we go on.

> *(Silence. The MĀLAMA PONO members gather up their things.)*

PALIKŪ: Thank you, Liko, for helping us tell the story.

MĀLIE: And you, Keanu, for listening to us.

KEANU: That's the end?

MAHINA: Every day the story changes, so the end could always come out different.

PALIKŪ: Depends on what we do—

MĀLIE: Or don't do.

PALIKŪ: We just wanted you to know how much that water means—

MAHINA: How everything we love depends on the water.

MĀLIE: What it means to Healani.

PALIKŪ: Aloha, Keanu.

MAHINA: Aloha, Liko.

MĀLIE: And mālama pono.

> *(The MĀLAMA PONO members exit. GINA hugs LIKO and waves to KEANU, then exits.)*

KEANU: *(takes LIKO's hand)* Come Uncle Liko, let's go home now.

SCENE 18

(The next day. From the house KEANU takes the water gourd and goes to the loʻi. He picks a taro leaf, puts it in the gourd, and walks to the bench, where HEALANI lies under her hospital sheet.)

KEANU: Mom?

HEALANI: Oh, Keanu. I'm so glad to see you.

KEANU: I brought you something.

HEALANI: Thanks, it's so pretty. You know, one day it will be yours.

KEANU: I want you to . . . I want to say I'm sorry for what I said.

HEALANI: And I'm sorry I haven't kept my promises.

KEANU: I, uh, want you to know, that I'm proud of you too, mom.

HEALANI: Oh, Keanu.

SCENE 19

(LIKO is working in loʻi as KEANU enters.)

LIKO: What you doing? I thought you was going soccer picnic.

KEANU: No, I'm not going.

LIKO: How come? You getting trophy.

KEANU: I have to go somewhere else.

LIKO: Where you going?

KEANU: I'm going up in the valley to help Mālama Pono block the road.

LIKO: What? Keanu, you just one small kid, you never know what's going happen at these things. You could be arrested, sometimes people get hurt, pretty bad too.

KEANU: They shouldn't take the water away from our valley.

LIKO: What your mother would say—

KEANU: I said, I'm going!

LIKO: *(beat)* Ho, you pa'akikī boy! *(pause)* Well, better I go with you.

KEANU: You don't have to.

LIKO: I not so old I cannot hold one sign.

KEANU: You want to?

LIKO: Maybe it's time, yeah?

> *(As LIKO and KEANU walk, BOY 1 and BOY 2 move in.)*

BOY 1: What, Keanu? You going protest?

BOY 2: You turn traitor?

BOY 1: You jerk head.

BOY 2: Who's that with you?

BOY 1: King Kamehameha?

KEANU: *(turns toward them, angry.)* Shut up you stupid—

> *(LIKO turns KEANU away. BOYS fade out.)*

LIKO: Eh, no bother with them. They only good for make noise.

> *(LIKO and KEANU stand alone at center. A VOICE comes over a loudspeaker.)*

VOICE: Okay everybody, we want you to remember this is a non-violent protest. That means, whatever they say or do, we never strike anybody, we never swear or insult them. Even if they hit us, we don't hit back. We stand.

KEANU: *(steps forward)* We came here today because we can stand up for ourselves. Because we can stand up for something we believe in. We came here today because everybody has the right to say stop, that is enough. We came here today to stand together. We link our arms tightly and we stand. Here, together.

> *(KEANU is joined by all cast members. There is the sound of rain and distant sirens.)*

CURTAIN

Victoria Nalani Kneubuhl was born in Honolulu of Samoan, Hawaiian, and Caucasian ancestry. She holds a Bachelor's degree from Antioch University and a Master's degree in Drama and Theatre from the University of Hawai'i. As a playwright, she has had plays produced, both locally and nationally. Her plays have toured to Britain, America, the Pacific, and Asia. Her work is published in several anthologies, and her own anthology: *Hawai'i Nei, Island Plays*, was recently published by the University of Hawai'i Press. She was named one of the Extraordinary Women of Hawai'i in 2001 by the Foundation for Hawaii Women's History and the Native Hawaiian Library of ALU LIKE, Inc. In 1996, she was the first theater artist to receive an Individual Artist Fellowship from the State Foundation on Culture and the Arts, and in 1994, she was honored with the Hawai'i Award for Literature.

Meredith M. Desha is a freelance writer and editor who also dabbles in the performing arts. She holds a Bachelor of Arts in English from Whitman College in Walla Walla, Washington, and is currently working toward her Masters of Arts in English with an emphasis in Creative Writing from the University of Hawai'i at Mānoa. She also serves on the Board of Directors of Kumu Kahua Theatre and is a member of improv comedy troupe Loose Screws.

John H.Y. Wat is an actor, director, writer and educator. He holds an MA in Speech Communication from the University of North Carolina at Chapel Hill and has completed coursework for the PhD in Performance Studies at Northwestern University. He serves on the Boards of Directors of Kumu Kahua Theatre and Bamboo Ridge Press. He teaches theatre and speech at the Mid-Pacific Institute School of the Arts.

Mary Mitsuda grew up in 'Aiea and graduated with a BFA from the University of Hawai'i at Mānoa. Her ti leaf monotypes were first shown in 2002 in exhibitions at The Contemporary Museum/First Hawaiian Center and at the Academy Arts Center at Linekona, Honolulu. In Hawai'i, her work can be seen in the Hawai'i State Art Museum, First Hawaiian Bank, Bank of Hawai'i, Nauru/Hawaiki Tower, Neiman-Marcus and in other public, corporate, and private collections. She lives and works in Pālolo.